Acknowledgements

First of all I would like to thank my bees, for teaching me about life. We now have a mutual understanding: I leave them alone, and they leave me alone. After writing this book, just before publishing, one lone bee got inside my suit, stung my lip, and shortly thereafter I found myself with a broken wrist to tend to. Beekeeping with one arm in plaster is not recommended.

Chapter 1
No Idea about Bees
19th April

Dear Shelagh,

    I went along to my first meeting with the Exeter Bee Association on Sunday, but I am afraid to write that it did not go well. From the moment I arrived, until I left some two hours later, it was not a good afternoon. Any thoughts about me keeping bees soon evaporated into thin air.

    The directions to the apiary sent to me via an email were obscure to say the least, 'off the main road and turn a sharp right before the White Horse Pub.' I sailed past the pub and for a further three miles, only later, I realized I had gone wrong. Trying to turn around was not easy, it was an extremely busy road. I then headed back towards the pub, and at the last minute before I went past the dam thing again, I turned a sharp left, without indication and with heavy, hard breaking, with a white van nearly up my arse, and with continues beeping from the van, and some hand gestures, I left the main road and drove up a narrow lane into the middle of nowhere.

After a few more lefts and rights by the directions given to me, I soon came to a road closed sign, which happen to be the road I needed to go down. I pulled over and sat looking ahead at the road closed sign and thought to myself, 'this is it, I shall turn around and go home.' But just as I turned the steering wheel to manoeuvre the car around, a brown, battered, old van came along; it stopped just in front of me. A man jumped out, moved the sign and drove through. I quickly followed close behind the van, and also followed it into a field, which was the 'first turning right' that I had written down on my piece of paper.

The van pulled up in front of a shed, and two men got out. I pulled up next to the van, turned my car engine off, and was about to get out of my car when one of the men came walking towards me shouting, 'park up the field.' He then turned around and went inside the shed.

I had a terrible feeling that this apiary meeting was not a good idea, and I really thought I should just forget the whole idea. But, I pressed on, more curious than anything else and went into the battered, tattered old shed.

The man, a grizzled old male, with harden, withered, features, not a smile of any sort nor any warmth, came through this fellow human being as he stood next to a wooden table making notes. 'I have just joined the Beekeepers Association,' I said, smiling up at him. He kept his hard look, 'you haven't been on our beekeeping course' he said grouchily. I shook my head no, 'I have got my bees coming in a couple of weeks,' I said, but more to a turned back, he had walked away from me. 'Anything I can do to help?' I asked, perhaps a little too keenly.

'Put those chairs out,' he said, pointing to a row of chairs in the shed, and 'light the gas burner for the tea.'

The chairs were the easy bit. I carried those outside in twos, but the gas burner I could not manage however hard I tried it would not light. I did not impress this man at all. He took over from me, not speaking, only grunting and lit the burner with ease. I felt foolish and went outside to sit down on a chair, and looked over towards the end of the field that was filling up fast with other cars arriving, and white suited people walking down towards the shed.

I introduce myself to faces I could only just see through heavy veils, there were nods and half-hearted smiles, but nothing more. I was on my own here, this was definitely a cliquey group, and novices like me were nothing more than a nuisance. I was bitterly disappointed because I had been so excited to go to my first Bee Keeping Association meeting to get to know other beekeepers, and perhaps learn from them, and more importantly find a hobby that made life more enjoyable.

The grizzled old man returned from the shed, he never introduce himself to me, I had no idea of his name, nor of the others around me. 'You had better get your suit on,' he said to me, 'you did bring it I hope?'

I looked around at the group of beekeepers all suited and booted, they sat in their seats all various shapes and sizes, dressed from head to toe in white suits. If I had been a member of the general public that had stumbled into this arena, I could have been forgiven for mistaken them as some sort of post-apocalyptic army, or perhaps a very sinister meeting of forensics, about to carve up a body. They certainly looked a scary bunch.

It was a beautiful hot summer's day, not a cloud in the sky, and as I walked behind the shed I could hear a low humming sound floating upwards towards me. The noise alerted me to thousands of bees. I quickly returned to my chair not wishing to disturb the bees at this early stage of my visit, and picked up my carrier bag with my brand new bee protective suit inside and casually removed it, and then attempted to put it on. I say attempted, because these suits are not straight forward, there are many bits and zips to them, and mine was brown not white. I had wanted a brown suit and not a white one, so as to blend in at the bottom of my garden, and not alarm my unsuspecting neighbours of my plans in beekeeping. They would certainly have spotted me dressed from head to toe in a white sort of space suit. Also my suit a smock top, it was much cheaper than the all in white suit. I had cut financial corners on my protective clothing, with assurances from my bee supplier that my bees were friendly.

I stood amongst the group of beekeepers wearing my suit, and was acutely aware of laughter. It was directed towards me. Red faced I realized that I had actually put my bee protective suit on the wrong way round. I was stuck, with zips and bits of netting getting in my way, and in my hair. A friendly beekeeper walked over towards me and helped me dress properly in my suit. But the grizzled man I first met just shook his head at me, and walked off disgusted behind the shed. I was at least dressed the part. 'All the gear with no idea,' as my son would say. I should have practice wearing my suit beforehand, but I did not realize that even a small thing like wearing a bee protective suit was going to be proven difficult.

The grizzled old man gestured for me to follow him. 'She hasn't been on a course,' he said to the other beekeepers. There were lots of muttering and head shaking. I had been named and shamed. I walked behind the group with my head hung low, aware that I was the odd one out in my brown suit. We went towards the shed, and then behind it, and then my first encounter with lots of bees. I was surprised to see twenty hives lined up, with thousands upon thousands of bees flying around the hives, and the air black with them.

I was beginning to think that ordering my forty thousand bees, twenty thousand in each hive, which were soon to be delivered within the next few weeks before I had done a course was not a good idea. The grizzled beekeeper did not need to say any further words, his facial expressions and his mannerism directed towards me, shouted out his disapproval. His sharp angry voice bellowed at me when I asked about the honey. 'Is that the honey?' I asked innocently as he removed a frame from one of the hives, he wore no gloves, he was after all a harden beekeeper. 'Don't go on about the honey,' he shouted. I really did feel at that point that I did not belong to this beekeeping group.

I was made to feel very small; in fact, humiliated would be a better word. I felt like the worst beekeeper in the world, and, doomed from day one. I was put into a group with two other woman, and a man without a bee suit, he had forgotten to bring his, which allowed me a smidgen of smugness since I did bring my bee suit. He was wearing his coat tied around his head and face, whilst wearing bright green washing up gloves on his hands. We were a motley, strange group, strangely dressed. I guess I fitted in straight away.

Before arriving at the apiary, I had only known bees and honey, nothing more, just two words associated with bees. My knowledge on bees was poor and limited to say the least. I had hoped in joining the Devonshire Beekeeping Association that I might learn. I soon realized that keeping bees was not as straight forward as I first thought.

As I entered the site of the hives, about twenty altogether, I felt alarmed at the numbers of bees flying around, thousands upon thousands of them, and here I was in the middle of them, dressed in a smock, veil and gloves. I did have the foresight to wear large Wellington boots with my trousers tucked inside. The sun belted down on me remorseless. I sweated inside my suit, and my gloves were sticky.

I was given the first task by the grizzled old beekeeper to inspect a hive. I peered into the thousands of bees after their hive top (technical term crown box) had been removed. I was handed a tool, and told to lift the frame out to inspect it. Inspect it for what I had no idea, but I went through the motions. I smoked the bees, just three puffs of smoke, to make them think their hive is on fire, and the buggers are supposed to dive down into their brood box to guzzle on honey and wait the danger out. But, of course there were still the brave bees on top, and I moved these between my fingers waiting to be stung. I carefully removed the frame that had been glued over by the worker bees with propolis, a hard sticky substance that bees use in their natural environment to make a hive. I then lifted the frame out of the hive, with thousands of swarming bees over it. The smoke was useless.

'Can you see the larva in the comb?' The beekeeper asked me. I replied yes, lying. Because I could not tell what was larva or wax, it all looked a mess to me. 'You have to be careful you don't lose the Queen Bee,' the beekeeper said, 'otherwise your hive will be lost without her.' I was informed that if a hive gets too crowded then the bees will swarm. Which means half your hive will disappear taking the old Queen Bee with them, leaving behind a new queen, that the worker bees would have been busy rearing with royal jelly. You can tell a queen cell on the frame, because it is much larger than the worker cells.

'These here,' said the beekeeper, 'these larger bees, they are the males, the drones, you don't want many of those, because they do nothing really useful in the hive. The males or the drones, fly around all day looking to mate with the worker bees, and come winter their wings are torn off by the females and they are thrown out of the hive to die.'

So basically a male bee does nothing but lie around all day drinking beer, smoking watching the football waiting for quick shag with a bee, and then die after they have had sex, which means they explode in the air, and then six weeks later even if they have not mated they still die a horrible death, because they are surplus to requirements.

Once they have mated, the Queen will lay up to half a million eggs in her lifetime which is usually three years, before she is killed off or replaced. The bee colony is quite a harsh environment to live in, ruthless, and without mercy. If you are not needed and you serve no purpose you die.

I examined three frames of larva, wax and honey, before moving out of the way for someone else to take over. I was hot, and looking forward to removing my bee suit. After another ten minutes the grizzled old beekeeper informed us that the bees were now getting angry because we had taken too long examining them and we need to close the hive down.

Thankfully we closed the hive, and I walked back to the shed and removed my bee suit. Only an angry bee had buzzed me, and followed me to my car. I waved my arms about like some sort of wild idiot, and then the bugger stung me on the arm.

Nursing my sore arm on the drive back home, I felt my very first introduction to beekeeping went well. However, as for the meeting with Devonshire Bee Association, it reminded me of my trials with the bell ringing lot at my local church in Newton St Cyres. I was feeling lonely when my son left home to go to university, so I joined the bell ringing group, thinking that this would be a good hobby, and a good way to get to out and meet new and exciting people.

I went to two bell ringing sessions, and not once on either of those occasions did anyone speak to me. I was astounded by the utter rudeness of the bell ringers, and what upset me more, was that they were all Christian church goers. I was ignored completely, left to sit on a ledge by the window in the tower, whilst four people of various ages pulled long ropes. They trooped in at eight in the evening on a Wednesday, and left at nine. A church mouse would have been notice more than I was. So, my hopes for meeting exciting and new people by joining the Bee Association failed miserably at the first post.

Chapter 2
Fifty Thousand Bees in My Car

21th April

Dear Shelagh,

Thank you for your letter, and the funny cartoons, I enjoyed them. Also thank you for your gift. I used it towards my Bee project.

I have now got my bees. I went and collected them from Holsworthy, about thirty five miles from here, near Bude on the North Devon Coast. I left at six thirty in the evening, to arrive at the Bee Farm, which is owned by a retired Police Officer and his wife. A very interesting couple, who told me that after a long time serving Police Officer, he felt he needed a complete change of lifestyle, far removed from the general public. So he went into bee farming.

Anyway I arrive at the bee farm, and the bee farmer took me to my two hives standing behind his house. They were to be transported back to my home in his nucleus box, (a small colony of bees that he has reared in a transport box). He would then come over to mine the following morning after the bees had settled into their new environment. He would transfer them to my hives. He could not do this straight away, as the bees need to orientate themselves where they are going to live, and besides throwing bees out of their home and into a new home and in a strange environment is not good for bees and makes them angry. No one likes angry bees. I have already been stung by an angry bee that followed me to my car on my very first meeting with Devonshire Bee association at their apiary, only a couple of weeks ago.

I made sure not to stand too close to the two hives; already being stung was not a pleasant experience so I preferred not to take any chances. I waited as the bee farmer removed one box to take it to the boot of my car. I looked inside the boot of my car as he lifted the lid of the nucleus box, and found to my horror about twenty thousand bees swarming around, not at all happy about being shut in and also moved!! I asked him whether taking the lid of the box was a good idea, but he said he had too because the bees would overheat, and besides he assured me they could not escape.

We walked back for the other box, but on my way back an angry bee that had been left behind when the first box was removed, decided to have a right go at me, and stung me on my temple. The sod, he had got caught in my hair and was buzzing very loudly next to my ear, then with the help of the bee farmer we managed to remove it, but not before she had stung me, only the female bees sting, the males (drones) have no stings. The pain from the sting on my temple was excruciating it made my eyes water. I tried to be brave, and smiled, and said 'right the next box now.'

I followed the bee farmer down to my car with bee box number two, the lid was removed, (a bee escape hatch had been closed over) and again thousands of angry bees hummed loudly. My head was throbbing, and the odd one or two were buzzing around the boxes, 'no need to worry about those,' the farmer said, 'they won't go far from their queen in the box.' I was not reassured with those words, and after the bee farmer apologised about my sting, saying that perhaps wearing a bee's suit might have prevented such an incident, I said my goodbyes and started the long careful drive home.

The drive back home was perhaps one of my more nerve racking drives, aware forty thousand bees, give a bee or two, were buzzing angrily in my boot, and if I were to have an accident, then any emergency services would be prevented access to my car and me, due to a lot of potential painful stings, and with at least forty thousand stings or more, I would not survive anyway.

It was dusk when I arrived home, and in the quiet and semi darkness I unloaded my two boxes one at time, and placed them at the bottom of the garden. I found carrying the buzzing boxes nerve racking. I very gingerly lent over the first box and opened the hatch to allow the bees freedom to escape if they so wish to do so. I moved on quickly to box number two and did the same thing, and then went indoors to have a much needed cup of tea, and nurse my now throbbing temple.

Sleep was not easy to come by, my head throbbed, my eye throbbed, and I could feel the side of my face swell up, and when morning came, and the bee farmer arrived, he looked on with sympathy at the right side of my face, which now looked as though I had fought nine rounds with a boxer. My eye was slowly closing. I put on a brave face, and also my bee protective suit and went down the garden to watch from some distance as the bee farmer removed the bees into my hives. He called me over to help, and with some reluctance I went over, nervous of the bees now buzzing nosily inches from my head, my nose and my eyes, only aware that a thin veil was keeping me away from other potential stings.

I have to confess that I no longer at this point had any confidence in being a bee keeper, and I also seriously considered asking the bee farmer to take the lot back with him. But, I hate to give in so easily, and very careful moved closer on his instructions to peer inside the hive which had now been filled with bees, his bees, in their new bee home, my bees. The only thing that stopped me running away was that I love all creatures, and these bees did not ask to be moved, or be kept, they were still living creatures with a highly order and organised life, they live by nature, and I felt I had a duty to take care of them as best as I could, with the little knowledge that I had. I owed it to them to learn quickly. My learning curve on beekeeping was going to be a sharp learning curve, or I will get stung and my bees die because when they sting me they die.

I offered the bee farmer a cup of tea, and a slice of my home made fruit cake, and we both sat in the sun watching the hives from a safe distance. 'What made you take up beekeeping?' I asked the friendly retired police officer. 'Because it is a relaxing way of making a living,' he replied, 'the rewards from the bees make it so worthwhile.' I was shattered from the lack of sleep from the previous night, and my head throbbed, 'relaxing' was not a word I would have associated with bees right at that moment.

The following day my face swelled up dramatically, I went along to my GP, who tapped on his desk with a long pencil and looked at me through his glasses. His face as most GP's was emotionless. 'So you have got bees, and they stung you?' he asked me. I replied yes, and then spent the next few minutes trying to convince the GP, and myself, how my new found hobby was going to help me, de-stress, and enjoy life. My GP handed me a prescription for medication for my swollen eye, my throbbing face, and advised me to always keep antihistamine tablets as a precaution for future stings. But, thankfully I was not advised to give up.

Chapter 3
My First Hive Inspection
27th April

Dear Shelagh,

It has been a week since my bees arrived. I have so far only ventured a little way down to the bottom of my garden, preferring to stay at a respectable distance from them, because my face is only just returning to normal, after the sting and very swollen down the left side. In my dreams I can still hear that frightening buzzing sound, of a very angry bee caught up in my hair determined to sting me and die. Honey bees die after they use their sting, it apparently rips their abdomen on humans, but if they sting an animal, they do not die, because animal's skins are softer. So humans do a lot of damage to bees by getting stung.

The following evening after my bees arrived I walked to the bottom of my garden; the sun was settling low over the distant moors. It was a peaceful and tranquil evening. I sat on the wooden bench ten feet away from the two hives. This was the respectable distance to stay clear, and not upset the bee colonies, according to my books. Then the buzzing started. At first it was not too close. I stood up carefully, but then the noise grew even louder.

I have been careful not to alarm my neighbours with my new hobby, but I have to say if they were watching from their windows then they would have seen me running wildly and quickly up the garden, waving my arms frantically. In shear panic I tore my coat off and threw it on the ground, and ran indoors, banging the door shut behind me. It was only later when I was leaving the house to take my dogs for their late evening walk, which I realized with horror that my front door key was somewhere down the garden, even possibly close to my hives, and twilight was fast approaching.

I knew that any hope of finding my front door key was useless in the semi darkness, but fortune was on my side, and only a few feet from the front door, my key lay on the path.

The next morning my sister rang and asked how my beekeeping was going. I did not lie to her, and said my bees were pretty much on their own at the moment, and that the stinging buggers could take care of themselves, because on my last two visit to see the bees, it had proved extremely painful. 'Besides,' I said, 'they have kept themselves going for thousands of years, I am sure they can manage without my help.' There was a long pause at the end of the phone, 'you said it was a good way to relax,' my sister said with a smugness to her voice, 'and what about your honey?' she asked.

'I don't like honey,' I replied, which was true. I have never enjoyed the stuff, far too sweet for me. 'I would be much happier if they produce Marmite,' I said.

Later on that afternoon I attempted to look at my bees, by watching a few feet away, (I was not going to give up that easy and be intimidated by the buggers), I was aware that my bees were rapidly producing and expanding quickly. I notice the amount of hive activity, which was a constant flow of bees in and out of the two hives, often the air thick with bees, and having read that rape seed in the fields around so close, was an easy source of pollen and nectar. These bees had an abundance of food source close to their hives, and they would need a super, which is an extra box on top of their hive so they can use the extra frames as their own food source to keep them going through the winter months.

You are supposed to put a queen excluder on top of the brood box, (the bottom hive where the queen lays her eggs and produces little bees) to stop the queen entering and laying in the super box. How this works is like a cattle grid, the workers can go through to the top box (the super) to produce honey, but the queen cannot get through because she is fatter and bigger than the other two types of bees.

I am not sure why you are supposed to add a queen excluder to the brood box to stop the queen going into the super. I have done some research on the internet to find out what this will achieve since you are not meant to take the honey anyway from the super at this point, because the bees still need it. There is no straight forward answer. Some say that you can take the honey and feed the bees sugar, which is diluted with water as a substitute, and that way you can start to produce your own honey early. But, I am not sure I want honey made from processed sugar and water. I much prefer to have the pure stuff, from pollen and nectar.

Other beekeepers say that this not fair to the bees, and that sugar and water is not good for them, and a poor substitute to replace their honey supplies, therefore you get poorly kept bees. Others argue that if you do put a queen excluder on the brood box to stop her going into the super then you don't get much honey either, so it is best left off. Instead of being called a queen excluder it is called a honey excluder.

I asked at the bee specialist equipment shop, where I buy my entire bee keeping equipment from, and they were the most helpful. I was told, put the queen excluder on, let the bees have their honey from that super, and once they have fill out those frames, then add another super, and if that gets filled (capped) then you can have that super full of honey for your own use, happy in the knowledge that at least the bees have plenty of their food source to keep them going through the winter months.

I placed one super on the first hive when my bees were first delivered, well I didn't do it, actually the bee farmer did it for me. I have to at some point add another super to my other hive which did not have a super on it at the time of the bees arriving. So this job was left for me to carry out and would be my first encounter with my bees on my own, and in my suit. There would be no support for me this time, and this was my first task.

The following morning whilst drinking my cup of coffee, I had in front of me my bible, a complete beginner's guide to bee-keeping. Since the arrival of my bees I have devoured a lot of reading material and watched a lot of you tube clips on bee-keeping. I have eaten, slept and dreamt about bees. I am on an extremely sharp learning curve. I was reading on how to add a super to the brood box. The pictures were helpful, and I felt fairly confident to have a go myself.

I had to first overcome my nerves. My stomach was in knots as I looked down the bottom of my garden at my two hives, where twenty thousand bees in each hive were housed, and happy. I was about to make them very unhappy by disturbing them, and if I took too long they would become agitated and angry bees. I made a mental note that according to the book the best time to work on your bee hives was at midday, when the worker bees, (the angriest ones) are away working, collecting pollen and nectar, and there would be fewer bees around.

The only problem I had was I had not told my neighbours about my new hobby. Both my neighbours on each side of me were out at work, and both due to return coincidently at around midday. I wandered down to the garden, and stood behind the bee hives, the time was eight thirty in the morning. The air was still cold, a slight mist hung in the air. My breath was captured on fine sprays. There were no bees in sight, instead a loud humming noise came from within my hives.

I made an instant decision and ran back into the house, grabbed my bee suit, and my smoker, and a few minutes later fully kitted, and smoker smoking, I went off carrying my super down to the bottom of the garden. I was doing everything the book said not to do. All the worker bees were still in the hives, it was far too cold for a bee to come out and gather nectar. But, my neighbours were out, and that was far more important to me then angry bees being disturbed early in the morning.

I carefully removed the lid of the first hive; a mass of crawling bees greeted me. I tried to stay calm, but felt my adrenalin rush kick in. I would be lying if I said I wasn't afraid. I was. There were thousands of potential bee stings, and I was about to disturb, anger them, and then for good measure stick my hand into their home.

I very carefully flicked a few remaining bees off their brood box, and then puffed a few puffs of smoke, they go down, but very quickly they return. To me smoke is useless, but according to most bee specialists it works, bees think their hive is on fire, dive down guzzle on honey and hide away. Not these bees. I smoked them, they dived down into the brood box, and then return a few seconds later.

I grabbed the super, flicked off more bees, and then slowly placed the super on top. I had left the queen excluder off. I wanted one hive with the queen excluder on, and one without, so I could compare the two. Both of my hives now had a super on top of their brood box. This would give them more room to grow, and hopefully stop them swarming, which they do when their hive becomes too crowded for them. Bees love crowds, but getting the balance right between what a bee think is just right, and not too crowded, to being overcrowded and then the buggers deciding to raise another queen, which means the old queen gets replaced and she then swarms off with half the colony.

I felt pleased with myself that I had managed to carry out my first task on my hives, and without killing or upsetting any bees in the process. I went inside the shed for a few minutes to calm down, my heart was racing, and I was sweating in a bee suit on a cold morning. I closed the shed door, and removed my suit. Only a few minutes later I rushed out without my suit on, aware that I was only a few feet away from my hives with thousands of pissed off bees from when I had disturbed them.

I had taken my smoker with me still smoking into the shed, and I was coughing and spluttering with all the smoke in the confines of a small shed. My eyes watered, my face stung, and my hair and clothes were stinking from smoke. I was also aware that I had not read anywhere in my books, on how to put out the smoker. I chucked it in an old wheelbarrow, alarmed at how fast the thing was catching fire. There had not been much rain for weeks, and everything was dry. I quickly threw the chicken's drinking water over the burning hay, making a mental note to learn how to do this in a more orderly, calm fashion.

I went back indoors, removed my clothing, had a shower, and another cup of coffee. I am yet to find this new hobby of mine relaxing and rewarding.

But, I had managed to work on my bee hives without getting stung, and when I went back down the garden later on that afternoon, my bees were busy flying in and out, and did not attack or follow me. I felt my confidence grow a little.

Chapter 4
The Bee Murderer
30th April

Dear Shelagh,

    I had planned on leaving the bees well alone since my last visit to them a couple of days ago, and placing a super on top of their hive, but yesterday evening, I had a phone call from a fellow bee keeper from the Devonshire Bee Association. He had been asked to 'buddy' up with me, to help and supervise me with my bees. I had my own doubts about this, because since my apiary meeting, where I had turned up like a fool with no knowledge whatsoever on bees. I have over the last few weeks read up and watched YouTube clips on bee keeping. Like a vacuum cleaner I had been hoovering up lots of information on bees. So, even though I had no real hands on experience with bees, my theory on those stinging little buggers was improving.

    I was slowly becoming aware that there are many different approaches to keeping bees. This had surprised me; because I had naïvely thought this was a straight forward past time. But, it was far from it. There was even a school of thought called 'natural beekeeping' whose philosophy was so different to the Beekeeping Association. They did not believe in smoke, protective suits, or checking on them. Even, the hives were completely different. The natural beekeeping had beautiful painted hives, very similar to the hand painted barges, with those distinctive colours and patterns, like the old fashioned wooden gypsy wagons. These hives were top down, meaning the bees were allowed to progress naturally as though in the wild, and to build their honey combs without the aid of wooden frames which already has honey and wire on them.

The bees natural instinct is to build downwards, but on hives called 'Nationals', bees are encouraged to build upwards, and by using brood boxes on the bottom, and placing supers on the top, with some bee keepers going as far as changing the frames around, with frames already filled out with honey and brood, and placing these in the supers, to encourage the workers to go upwards, the bees are going against what is natural for them.

Also in 'natural beekeeping', bee keepers are not encourages or taught to carry out weekly checks on their hives, instead, the beekeeper is told to leave them alone, and only towards the end of August when the bees have finished their extensive foraging, only then, if there is any honey left over after first making sure that the bees have sufficient food for the winter, then it is ok to remove some honey.

But, in the Devonshire Beekeeping Association, their views are quite the opposite to the natural way. They reminded me of Crofts, the dog show, where poorly interbred dogs, are displayed around an arena, and judged, and for the winner large sums of money given as prizes. I felt the Devonshire Beekeeping Association had similarities in their working practices, prizes for the most honey, and named in their glossy magazine.

The Bee Association have bees paraded around in a circle, (in a box) and judged. There are prizes for the best queen rearing, and big money to be made on rearing queens. With queens and queen cells destroyed, pinched or scrapped out, if they do not come up to scratch. Bees are engineered to what the beekeepers want, and not what the bees want. The same for Crufts when dogs are breed and interbreed, with horrific deformities, but according to the judge, these dogs who have problems breathings, walking, or even able to see in some cases, are judged the correct way, and again prizes are given for the dog owner who has managed to breed to strict regulations. Dogs then suffer, and cats, who have similar breeding programmes, and to my horror bees are treated the same way. Humans meddling around in nature, genetically engineering for their own programmes. Shocking.

So, when the phone call came from a fellow beekeeper from the association, I was not sure what to do. I mean here I was a novice in a hobby, or whatever one wants to call it, when it comes to keeping bees, and quite frankly I could do with all the help I could muster. But, even so I had my reservations, and I was not keen to allow this man to come over and see my bees, or worse, even fiddle or meddle with them.

I have been reading lots of literature on bees, and watched many video clips on bee keeping, and normally, I would have been extremely grateful for this man's help. But, now I was not too sure. I was worried his ways in keeping bees, would not be compatible to mine, which is leave alone, and let nature do its thing.

I was leaning more towards the natural beekeeping approach, and strongly believed that man does not have the right to interfere with nature. We humans have participated so much in destroying many creatures, many to extinction, through hunting. Bees are already on the decline due to their lack of natural habitation for them to live, and to be able to extract the pollen and nectar they require to survive. The over use of pesticides killed off lots of bees, with many on the brink of extinction. Over development on our green belts has also led to a decline in our bumble bee, as well as the honey bees.

How can a bee get its nectar and pollen from tarmac and bricks? How can the bee build its hives naturally in old trees when trees are being cut down to make way for new developments? And without bees who will help to pollinate our vegetation? Humans would become frighteningly on a downward spiral for their own food source, unless that too is artificially created in labs.

Much of honey is mass produce, usually created artificially by substituting the nectar and pollen for boiled water and syrup. So, I was not thrilled to read about the Devonshire Bee Association and their not so natural ways, and not so happy to invite one of them to come and inspect my hives.

I had a lapsed in my own judgement when I said 'yes' to the man from the association. I did not have the confidence to say 'no' to his help, and invited him to visit my hives the following day.

Instantly regretting my decision, but not able to back out I waited for this man to arrive. He was due to be at my home at three pm, and when three pm came and went, and it was nearer four o'clock, I breathed a sigh of relief, thinking he was not going to turn up. But, a sharp knock on my door alerted me to the beekeeper.

I had wanted to keep my bees on a low radar, especially from one of my neighbours, who I do not get on with. I am not sure why we do not speak to each other. I tried and was ignored, and you cannot go around forcing people to speak and like you. So, we neighbours muddle on side by side without speaking to each other, although one day I did take a parcel for her. But, sometime later when she knocked on my door, and I handed her parcel over to her, not a word was spoken on either side. I waited for her to thank me, or even ask for her parcel; instead she stood there, not a word, just waving a bright orange ticket with instructions written on it to knock on my door to retrieve her parcel, from a kind neighbour who took it in for her. But there was nothing on her face, it was grim, with every crease pulled tight on pale skin, and a thin mouth zipped shut, and with hard, dark, eyes that stared back at me. What is more worrying is this person works in the caring profession. It like having the grim reaper peering over you whilst washing you down.

So it was with this in mind, me wishing to keep a low profile that I was somewhat alarmed to see a beekeeper dressed from head to toe in white, wearing a veil, carrying a large box and a smoker in his hand, standing on my front step in full view of everyone. I ran outside quickly and ushered him around the back, hoping he had not been seen.

'This is my box of beekeeping tools,' Stephen the beekeeper said. I looked at the bottom of my garden where my two bee hives were quietly set, without any disturbance from humans, allowing the bees to fly in and out, going about their daily business. Now, confronting me was a man determined to get his hands on my bees.

'They do not need any sort of checks,' I said, 'they are quite happy down the bottom of my garden. I was just hoping you could take a look from a distance to see if my super that

I fitted was on properly.' The beekeeper was not listening to me, he had turned his back on me and was busy lighting the smoker, and within a few minutes fierce smoke bellowed from his little canister. I was alarmed to see such smoke, when all I wanted was a quick look from about ten yards, something I had frequently done since I had bought my bees, and they certainly did not bother me, and appeared quite happy to fly around me.

Stephen the beekeeper picked up his box and stomped down my garden. I quickly put my bee protective suit on and followed him. He swiftly opened up my first hive, smoking the bees aggressively, and as usual nothing happens, the bees still buzz around. They drop away for a few seconds but then soon appear, angrier then ever that someone was interfering with them.

I watched helpless and alarmed, children were playing in my neighbour's garden, and I had read in my bee keeping bible, it was not a good idea to upset the neighbours, and it was best to inspect your bees in the quiet of the evening, when no-one was around. But, this man from the association had his own agenda. He pulled the hive apart, taking out the frames one by one, tilting them this way and that. 'Ah, this one has honey. This one has brood, and worker bees on it, and a few drone cells.'

The point of this inspection I failed to understand. It made no sense whatsoever, apart from intruding into the bee's lives. 'You need to do this at least once a week,' Stephen said to me, as he walked around to my second hive. 'You really don't need to inspect this one,' I said to him, but it was too late, smoke was puffed into the hive, angry bees buzzed around him, and he took the frames out once again one by one. 'You have a queen cell,' Stephen said excitedly. 'You need to get rid of this to stop them swarming,' he was pulling the cell apart with his hive tool (a metal tool to prise frames apart).

Alarmed at the destruction of something naturally occurring, I reached over and stopped him, taking the frame off him. 'Enough now,' I said firmly, 'the bees are angry.'

Stephen put the hive roughly together and killed lots of bees in the process by squashing them. I was shocked at how many dead bodies lay around the hive. I walked away disgusted, and thankfully he followed me back up the garden, and as we walked ten to twenty bees followed him, buzzing him angrily. Stephen clapped them together in his hands, their dead bodies dropping to the ground. I was upset at the treatment my bees were receiving from him.

Ten minutes later after one angry bee was still buzzing and dive bombing Stephen's head, the bee was killed between Stephen's hands, and it too lay squashed outside my shed.

I look dismally around me as lots of tiny bee bodies lay crumbled, fallen to the ground dead, doing only what was natural to them, and that was defending their hives. 'Oh a few dead bees don't make any difference,' Stephen said, as I picked up the dead bees and placed them in a pile on top of the garden table. 'There are thousands more still around,' he said.

To me that was not the point, he had missed the point of bee keeping, which was to look after bees, take care of them, as much as nature did in the wild, and not to kill them because they buzz you. Why kill something even if it is small and part of thousands of others, it was still not right or gives you the right to kill a living thing, especially if it is defending its home.

I did not bother to invite Stephen into my home for a drink, a coffee or tea, instead I was relieved to see the back of him, and when he finally placed his bee box and kit inside the boot of his car, and drove off, I waved a sigh of relief.

I returned to my garden, and began slowly collecting dead bees from my patio area and placed them all in a row, sadden by the sight of their little legs with their sacks loaded, where they had been collecting yellow rape seed oil pollen and nectar from the fields, and were returning home laden with food for their hive, only to be disturbed in such a brutal manner, and killed in such a brutal manner, and here their crumbled dead bodies lay in a row. There seemed a lot of bee bodies, and I counted thirty. Their yellow sacks of precious nectar and pollen would not be used, all their hard work for nothing, their short lives shorten even quicker.

'Never again,' I thought to myself, 'will that man or any other person from the Devonshire Bee Association be allowed near my bees again.' I was also worried that my bees would become angry bees, not able to forget their brutal encounter with this Devonshire Bee Association member. I walked down to the hives and stood a few feet away like I use to do, but within seconds I was chased by another angry bee. So I left well alone, and a few days later in the quiet of the evening, when the sun had set, and without my suit. I collected the remaining dead bees, the bee man had killed. I was shocked to see their hives littered with dead bodies. When I had worked on them, I had not killed one. But, now my hives looked like a mass bee grave. Under the roof, I could make out half dead bees, squashed by the heavy roof.

After clearing away the dead bees, I went indoors to have a much needed cup of tea, when my mobile phone beeped. It was a text message from Stephen the bee man. 'I can't wait to come over and do some queen searching for you,' it read. I pressed the delete button, the bee murderer would not be returning to my hives. I would have to get by on my own knowledge gleaned from books, carefully selected, and by more importantly by the bees themselves.

Chapter 5
Bee Burial

1st May

Dear Shelagh,

There was a loud knocking on my door, and when I answered it, my friend Colin who shares the same compassion as me when it comes to all creatures on planet earth, stood on my doorstep holding a plastic see through bag laden with dead bees. I explained to Colin about how these dead bees came about, whereby, Colin uttered a few words, 'don't let that bastard come back San,' he said, and then added, 'what shall I do with these?' Holding a bag of dead bees.

I looked at the bag full of lifeless bodies, 'bury them please Colin,' I said, and without another word Colin walked down the garden towards the shed, and a few minutes later armed with a shovel he proceeded to dig a hole, and lay the bees to rest.

It was a few minutes later, even before Colin had time to return the shovel to the shed, when the chickens who had been eyeing Colin's digging a few feet away, descended upon the little mound and proceeded to dig it up, chittering in utter delight at their find, dead bees which they consumed with gusto. The reason why my bees are fenced in is to stop the chickens getting to my bees and picking them off at their hive doors.

Colin turned around and watched the grave dug up. He stood for a few seconds, shook his head in disbelief and walked back towards the shed. The bees demolished, now inside the chickens, I realised that perhaps tomorrow I would be eating the bees through the chicken's eggs, which I would collect and cook. 'Everything is recycled,' I thought to myself.

I spent the rest of the day watching the hives from a respectable distance; I would not go too close. I wanted to give them time to recover from their ordeal. Also I had read that bees which have been disturbed would be set back at least twenty four hours in their colony.

The rapeseed oil was in full yellow flower and the bees were making a bee-line for it. They use the same direction each time to collect the pollen and nectar, hence the word bee-line. It was fascinating to watch these little creatures who ignored my own selection of flowers, that I had recently specially planted to encourage them to pollinate, instead the little buggers flew directly towards the rapeseed field some hundred yards away. They flew past my own flowers. Bees are opportunists and much prefer to collect nectar and pollen from a large source, instead of flying from flower to flower, shrub to shrub a few distances apart, instead they prefer a large crop area where they can quickly fill their sacks with pollen and nectar in one go and return quickly to the hive. The humble bumble bee, flies from flower to flower, but honey bees, prefer lots of flowers in one area.

My father had suggested that I plant an assortment of flowers to attract my bees, but my flowers were attracting an abundance of bumble bees, and butterflies, which pretty much do the same thing as the honeybee, in that they all pollinate.

It was later that evening when my mobile phone beeped at me, it was another text message from Stephen the bee murderer. I reluctantly read his text message, much preferring to ignore him, and try and look after the bees without his help. But, his message brought a smile to my lips. The message read, 'I have been down to my bee hives nearly every day this week, and yesterday my wife washed my bee-suit. I put it on this morning, but the veil across the face has gone slack by the hot wash, and when I went to visit my bees wearing my clean bee suit, the veil flapped against my face with a lot of angry bees clinging to it. I got stung on my face, lip and ear.'

The words 'sweet justice' sprang to mind. His bees had been unnecessarily disturbed nearly every day last week by Stephen the bee man, and the bees had manage to get their own back on him, by waiting for an opportunity. The opportunity was not long in coming when his wife, who had little knowledge on beekeeping had simply taken his suit, and unknowingly not realize that you do not wash a bee suit because the veil will soften in the hot water and lose its ability to stay rigid and keep away from the face. Of course when angry bees fly up onto your veil it can be quite alarming, but usually safe in the knowledge that your veil is away from your face brings comfort that you won't get stung.

The picture of horror on Stephen 's face must have been pure joy to the bees, having been poked, prodded and their queen cells destroy, they seized their opportunity for pay back, by flying up to the veil, landing on it, and feeling the soft skin beneath their tentacles, have stung their prey.

I have been stung twice, and the pain varies. My first sting was only a kiss, a warning, just a light touch. I did not realize at first that I had been stung; it was only a few minutes later that my arm hurt, a slight pain, like having a vaccination. It was a few hours later that my arm started to throb, then swell up, but the pain was bearable, more of a nuisance. My night's sleep was disturbed, mainly because I lie on my right side, and my arm had been stung on the right arm, and when I turned over without thinking about it and lay on the side that had been stung, it then hurt like hell, forcing me to turn over.

The second time I was stung, which was on the side of my forehead and close to my left eye, the pain was intense and immediate, it was as though my head had been hit by a red hot poker. The pain even brought tears to my eyes, and sent a shock through my body. I was expecting to be stung good and proper the second time, because the bee had chased me when its hive had been moved to the boot of my car. I heard the close buzzing sound around my head, and my worst fears realized when the bee got tangled in my hair, it was angry, and the noise was close to my ear. Then suddenly pain shot through my body.

The area around the temple does not have a lot of protection, so the pain was searing and immediate. I knew straight away that this was going to bad, but how bad I had no idea until later that night, in fact in the early hours of the morning, when I woke up and tried to open my eye. It would not open, and I felt the side of my head throbbing in terrible pain. I struggled out of bed, and with my one good eye peered at my mobile phone and looked at the time, which was two thirty in the morning. I walked into the bathroom and had a shock, my face was swollen, it had ballooned up, and I looked like I had been in a boxing match and come off a lot worse. It had been one single bee that had caused this.

I felt around on my temple and felt the lump and a piece of the sting sticking out, and too my horror realized that the bee sting had been left in my head. I was unable to get the remaining bee sting out, as I could not see what I was doing.

It was early morning when I finally went to my GP who said that I had had a nasty reaction, and was told to take antihistamine tablets. I was also given an injection straight away and given a nasal steroid spray. The GP's words were, one of a warning, and he told me to be aware, in that I can have an allegoric reaction to bee stings.

It took two days for my face to calm down and the lump on my head where I had been stung another two weeks to go down. So, I do treat my bees with respect, and try not to disturb them unless I am required to do so, like putting another super on top of their brood box. But, I work quickly, carefully, and try to be less intrusive as I can, showing my bees a lot of respect. Unlike Stephen, who wades into his hives (and mine) with extreme gusto, with no respect, and with no care, he liberally uses his smoke, he does not bother to remove the remaining bees before placing the super back, therefore squashing a whole lot of bees, and of course the bees are going to be angry when he squashes queen cells, and drone cells, when the bees have been working dam hard to make them. He deserves to be stung, but unfortunately those bees that stung him would have died, and no doubt he crushed many more.

20th May 2017

Heating up in Dubai

Dear Shelagh

I have been in Dubai the last two weeks visiting my son, and left my bees to their own devices. I use to leave

Chris's apartment at 9.30 am to walk the short distance to the supermarket, it registered 34 degrees at that time of the morning and usually hits 42 degrees about 11 am. I would walk to the shop alright, but on my return journey it would start to heat up quickly, and I struggled with my shopping to get back to Chris's flat. The sun was relentless, and the hot air made it difficult for me to catch my breath. The worse part was when I did arrive at Chris's apartment block, I then had 7 floors to walk up in the stair well, which was just as stifling or perhaps worse than outdoors, because of the build up of hot air in an airless building. I hate lifts, so I always take the stairs, but when I reached the fifth floor, I had to sit down on the stairs to get my breath, and the lights went out, so I was sitting in pitch darkness, in the stifling heat, with my bags of shopping and two more flights to go!!

Once I arrived at his flat I unloaded my bags into the fridge, nearly everything goes into the fridge, even my medicine. I left the butter out for only a couple of minutes the other evening when I was cooking, and when I returned, it was liquid!! It no longer looked like butter. It was so far removed from a block of butter.

To get some respite from the heat I spent most of my time sitting with my feet dangling into the water at the outdoor swimming pool situated just above Chris's flat. The heat forcing me to get into the pool, but I did manage a few laps, the water was warm, no surprise there, because it soon heats up. I got carried away with my swimming, mainly because the water was much preferable to the searing heat I would have to walk into as soon as I left the pool.

I would feel myself burning, and with extreme reluctance I would get out of the pool and walk back into the apartment. After washing my hair, I would stand for few seconds on Chris's balcony whilst my hair dried in the hot air, and then peg my washing out on their airer on the balcony, but the sun bleaches it, so I have to keep an eye on the washing, as my blue tee-shirt will return to me white, or a very strange off blueish sort of white, bleached by the searing sun. Oh the pegs, on Chris's balcony were full of sand, and because they were plastic they had melted!!! The pegs were indeed a very strange shape, not at all peg shaped. The pegs had been twisted into a strange plastic mess by the heat.

I had no choice but to sit with the air con on and when I opened the balcony door I would have to close it quickly as the intense heat pours into the apartment, unlike the UK whereby, we close our doors in winter because the cold air comes in, here you close the doors and windows because the hot air pours in. Us humans are never satisfied with the weather.

If you want to get a feel of the heat here in the desert of Dubai, stick your head in an oven for a few minutes, it is very similar. I would often feel like sticking my head in the fridge.

The fruit in Dubai is ripe and full of taste, I suppose it does not have far to travel to the shops, unlike the UK when the fruit is forced to ripen after a long journey. I often made a fruit salad for Chris to take to work, and one morning I had an email from him, which read;

'Hi Mum, the blubberies you put in with my fruit sald this morning where covered in hairy green mould. Becareful with them. I think I must have eaten about 4/5 of them before I noticed something was wrong. Probably have a dogey stomach later. x'

I replied to Chris's email about his dogy blueberries, with the following email;

'Hi Chris, the blubberies were ok last night, so must have gone off quickly this morning. I did check them over to make sure before I washed them (each one of them), and no hairyness on them. I don't think 4 or 5 hairy blueberries will do much harm. They have all gone now, because I finished the rest off. I also think from the time you took them out of the fridge to the time you eat them, the hairyness must have occurred somewhere along the corridor to the lift from you flat, and then across the car park into your car, then out of your car and whilst you walked into your school, somewhere at that point, in the hot humid air of 42 degrees, the blueberries transformed into hairy creatures. So beware, and be warned, that in future, if you take blueberries out into the hot desert heat, they will turn into hairy little monsters.

However, I did do some research, and eating small bits of mouldy fruit is ok. But, blueberries do not enjoy the desert heat of Dubai. Lots of love mum xxxx'

Tara returned from her holiday in India on Tuesday morning and offered to take me to the shops, for a moment I did think about walking, but after my last morning's walk, I decided to accept her offer. It was 9.30 am, when we drove over to the supermarket, and the car's temperature outside registered 38 degrees, the hottest part of the day was yet to come.

I bought some eggs, bread and butter, and then Tara dropped me off before heading into down town (the tall big buildings area). Again I thought about walking back to Chris's apartment, mainly because in the UK I always walk, and enjoy doing so, but as I wanted the eggs to be fresh and not hard boiled by the baking sun, and for the bread to be fresh and not burnt to a crisp, and also for the butter to still look and be in the shape of butter, and not a runny, oozing, mess in the bottom of my carrier bag. It was with this in mind that I decided to accept the lift back to the apartment, grateful that I did not have to trudge back wearily in the searing desert heat.

I did however walk up the stairs, and only just made it back into the apartment before the butter turned to liquid, due to the intense heat in the stairwell. The butter was starting to drip and not look like a block of butter, but a soft ply type mess. I put the items in the fridge and then went up the pool for my morning swim before my head heats up in the pool (it got seriously heated yesterday).

The other morning when I went to the pool area I left my flip flops near the table and when I had finished swimming in the pool, I had to endure walking painfully across the baking hot surface to collect my flip flops. My feet burned like buggery until I placed them in my flip flops.

So as not to repeat that performance I decided to place my flip flops by the edge of the pool. The time was 10.30 am in the morning, the midday burning sun had not yet arrived. I did about half and hours swim in the warm water, my head burning nicely, the rays of the sun penetrating my scalp. The fear of sun stroke forced me to give up, so it was with reluctance that I got out of the pool only to find my flip flops had melted!!!!

I hopped from toe to toe, foot to foot, over a burning surface until I reached the door into the air conditioned building. I have since stuck my flip flops in the fridge next to butter!!! And, stuck my own head that got burnt, also in the freezer compartment. I then rinsed my swimwear out, that only consist of a blue tee-shirt and some old knickers my mother gave me. I did not have a swimsuit, my old one had got too tight for me. I then hung my tee-shirt and knickers out to bake, using twisted pegs to keep them from blowing off the balcony. My once blue tee-shirt is now nearly white, and everything gets covered in fine sand within seconds of being on the balcony. It is after all a desert.

Later that evening Chris treated me to a pedicure and a manicure, carried out by a young Indonesian lady. She spent and hour on my hands messaging, cutting and painting my nails, and then an hour on my poor blistered feet. It felt like pure luxury and the whole thing cost twenty five pound for the lot.

After my procedure, I left Tara to get hers done and I took a walk across the road to the shop, (there is a small shop which is expensive but handy for an odd item or two, located in a large apartment block opposite Chris's apartment) to buy some milk.

I did my usual, which was to walk down the stairs, I just hate lifts, and walk across the sandy road, only to be met by a very skinny black kitten. As you know I am a softy when it comes to animals, and I tried to ignore this kitten, but I must have a homing instinct for animals in need. I left the cat outside the shop next to the restaurant area. I found the milk, and then against my better judgement I bought some cat food.

I returned to the heat outside, the air was still humid even though it was nearly ten pm, the nights are nearly as bad as the days in Dubai, only to find the kitten being chased off by the staff at the restaurant. I went and sat on a wall opposite the restaurant and waited, the staff looked across at me. I held up my cat food and shook it, and one of the staff shouted, 'your cat?' I nodded 'yes,' whereby the kitten was picked up and dumped beside me. The poor skinny thing, looked up at me and meowed. I was being observed closely by the restaurant staff. My son had warned me that living in Dubai you do not do anything to upset the local people, and to act normal, because their laws are strict, and animals are treated as pests, and vermin.

I slowly bent down and opened my packet of cat food and tipped it out onto the pavement. I then sat back and watched the kitten eat hungrily. The staff from the restaurant watched me, the people dinning watched me, all locals, no ex-pats watched me. Whilst the kitten eat, I got up and slowly walked away, and towards Chris's apartment, hoping the kitten would not follow me.

I realized later when I returned to the apartment that my nails which had been painted red and had been massaged and cleaned with oils, had bits of cat food stuck in them, and the red nail vanished had been scrapped off where I had been trying to remove the cat food from the packet. In fact my hands stunk of cat food, and also my toes were covered in sand. So that was a waste of twenty five pounds, that only lasted less than ten minutes. But, still I did get to feed a hungry kitten.

All twelve days I spent in Dubai were baking hot, and I sort of fell into a routine whilst Chris was at work. In the mornings I would walk to the shops to buy food to cook the evening meals, and yesterday morning when I left to walk to the shops, I stepped into a searing heat that instantly took my breath away. By the time I had reached the supermarket some fifteen minutes walk away, I could feel myself burning up. It was hotter than ever before. I sort of half staggered into the air condition building only to find myself light-headed, with my head starting to spin. I had raced to beat the sun before it had risen too high, but the sun had won, it beat me, leaving me feeling completely exhausted and drained.

I tried to shop, whilst all the time, feeling quite faint, and the last thing I wanted to do was pass out in the shop and get taken to a hospital. The hospitals are normally situated in skyscrapers, tall big buildings. I certainly did not wish to wake up and find myself in an awkward situation of being in one of those dreaded high buildings and pass out again!! So I fought it, until I arrived at the check out, where I stood behind a lady wearing the hijab, with only her eyes showing.

The woman must have sense my plight, and asked in me in perfect English if I was ok. I replied that I had walked to the shops and underestimated the heat, she told me to follow her. I did so. The woman had a small child with her and was heavily pregnant. When we arrived at a very new and posh car, but rather battered with dents and bumps all over it, with the side door completely bashed in, the woman told me to get into her car and she would give me a lift back home.

The woman looked at me, whilst I tried not to stare too hard at the beaten up new car. 'Oh,' she said rather sheepishly, 'I have had two accidents recently.' I thought to myself, I have a choice here, crawl back in the sand on my hands and knees to the apartment, hoping the sun would not get to me, or catch a lift in a strangers car whose driving capability was not reassuring.

I chose the car. Once in the car, she removed her veil covering her face, and said she would like to drop me off at the apartment and asked me for directions to get there. A few scary minutes later with my eyes shut, the woman's driving was quite something, I arrived at Chris's apartment. I thanked her, and then proceeded to climb the seven stories, (I just hate lifts) which was hard work!!

I was so relieved to reach the apartment, and sit in the cool room with the air con blasting away, but I also took time to reflect on the kindness of this stranger who had gone out of her way to take me home. Would this have happened in the UK I asked myself, and the answer was probably no. After a few minutes I went up to the pool where I stayed until my hands and toes were so wrinkled forcing me to reluctantly leave the water. Later that evening when Tara came home from work, she had left in the morning the same time as me and had offer to drive me to the shops but I refused saying the exercise was good for me, she said that the outside temperature had been hotter than usual in the morning than any other mornings so far, and had registered 42 degrees!!

So I had not beaten the sun, it had got up early and burned the hell out of me as I trudge wearily across the white sand to the shops, with the breeze blasting hot air just to make it even more difficult. Its the catching of my breath that makes it extremely hard work in the heat. Chris told me not to walk to the shops because it is far to hot, but I thought I am older than him, and his mother and I know best, so I had ignored his advise and walked to the shops. I should have listen to him.

The nights were no easier, the heat made sleeping difficult. I did try sleeping with Chris's balcony doors open, but the hot air blows in like a fan oven. I often gave up on that idea and settled for the air conditioning, which is not always a good way to sleep, the noise is loud, and the cold air blasting away can force me to shiver and reach out for a jumper, which is tucked away at the bottom of my suitcase waiting for my return to the unpredictable British weather.

I spent my last morning swimming up and down the pool, only to stop now and again to gaze across the desert in one direction and the marina in the other. It was during one of my rest stops, that involved me leaning on the edge of the pool with my body submerged in the waters, when I heard a strange noise and tuned around, normally there is no-one else up on the pool area so early in the mornings, so the sound rather like a dog yapping in the distance, caused me to stop and look across the roof tops. Dogs are not a common sight in Dubai, in fact on my last two visits to Dubai, I have seen only one dog, and that was in the desert when I went on a cycle ride.

The sound was above me, I noticed a dove sitting on the sun canopy post. There is no sun canopy nor shade, because Chris said the noise when the wind blew the canopy kept him awake at night, like living on a marina with the sails banging away against the side of the boats. So it was, that one person in the whole block of about four hundred people, manage to get the canopy taken down, and thus removing any shade or respite from the sun, for the rest of the residents living in the building, but at least Chris does get his sleep now.

The Dove perched high above me, made a strange barking sound, so strange, but a beautiful bird. I have often wondered how the wildlife manage to survive in the desert heat, without food or water. I took my books on bees with me, and whenever I had the opportunity, I would whip my books out and squint in the harsh sun and read. I was learning about the different types of bees in the world, with wonderful exotic names in Latin, similar to the names of plants, for example, Colletes halophilus.

Armed with some knowledge on bees I am now on the lookout for the differing species of bees, and I did wonder if there were any living in Dubai. So far I have not seen any, a bit like dogs, even if they do exists then they were hidden out of sight. I did see flies, lots of those.

I was however, surprised to find local Devonshire honey in the small shop under the apartment block. I casually glanced across the shelves of honey, until my eyes were drawn to a familiar jar. I picked it up and examined it and was utterly surprised to read it came from Newton Abbott, a few miles away from me. Here it was on the shelf in an obscure shop in the middle of the desert, not even in one of the main shops down town.

I took with me two jars of local honey for my son to try, worrying if they would make the flight without smashing and covering all my clothes in a sticky mess, and also if they would get through the strict customs. My jars of honey were so thoroughly bubble wrapped that when I placed them in my suitcase, I thought they looked like small round bombs which were not ideal for travelling to the Middle East.

I have a fear of high ceilings so my bee book was quite useful when I finally reached Dubai and whilst waiting for my son to collect me from the airport, he had been caught up in heavy traffic and was late. Instead of thinking about the high ceiling above me, I could instead read up on bees, and learn that the urban honey bee survives and produces better honey then bees hived in the countryside.

This is due to their natural habitation being eroded to create more efficient farming, and wild flowers not so common due to the pesticides used over decades of farming. Therefore, brown sites are better habitat for bees then green land. The author Dave Goulson who wrote 'Bee Quest' even suggested that protesting about green belt development would not do the wildlife much harm even if the land were built on the green belt. It would be better he argued, to develop on the green belts, and use the brown belts that have been left for nature to take over, and therefore, have not been subjected to harsh over farming and pesticide use, and to keep these brown belts as nature reserves for bees and wildlife to thrive.

Reading the chapter on urban bees surprised me, there I was thinking that my bees were lucky buggers because they have all those lovely fields around me, when in fact the urban bee especially the bees living in London, have more opportunities to sample flowers of all different varieties, and not at risked of being poisoned from pesticides. How naive I had been. Before I left Newton St Cyres I had watched the farmer driving his tractor spraying the fields, where my bees had been collecting pollen and nectar. I had no idea that this could be dangerous for them.

Later that evening my last night in Dubai, Chris and I walked along Kite beach, the public beach, and bought a drink from a stand, mine was pure sugar cane, and Chris had a fresh strawberry drink. It was a wonderfully relaxing evening as we sat and watch the sun go down. It slips away quickly here, and then all the lights spring into life around us on the tall skyscrapers, with the Burj Khalifa (the world's tallest building) lit up. A magnificent sight. I am more relax with the high buildings this trip, and sort of getting use to them, but I am also looking forward to returning to my hard working girls, those bees, and hope they were doing ok without my weekly inspections, not that I would do the recommended weekly inspections, and annoy the hell out of them and make them angry.

    According to my Bee Quest book, bees have been around for one hundred million years, and have done quite well without the interference of man. I shall of course take a peep inside their super, and check whether there is any spare honey for me on my return. But, I will not prod and poke them unlike the Bee Association recommendations. We could learn a lot from bees.

Chapter 6
Angry Buzzing Bee
23rd May

Dear Shelagh,

I manage to check my bees today. The first time since I have arrived back in Devon. The weather has been appalling since my return to Devon, and I have read that bees get very grumpy if the weather is not good, they hate storms, and torrential rain, and the weather has been doing both.

With the weather taking a turn for the better and warm sunshine pouring over the apiary, I thought I would take my chance and visit them. Now my visits have a purpose, and today I wanted to check how far they had been working on their frames. There are ten frames in the super and if they are nearly completed, that is working on them to make honey, then bees need more space and it is important that I give them that space by either adding another super on top of the super already in place. This makes my hives quite large, which would consist of a brood box (the bottom box where bees make bees and store their food), then a super on top of the brood box with a queen excluder on top, which stops the queen laying eggs in that box, because otherwise the colony will get too big and perhaps swarm. Because the queen cannot lay her eggs in the super this then becomes the honey box, whereby the bees make honey for their winter stores.

If the bees complete the super with honey early in the year and before autumn, then I can remove a few frames of honey for myself, whilst making sure that the bees can add to their super and store honey for their winter survival.

I got myself suited up, got the smoker going and armed with my tool to remove the super box, I was ready for an inspection. I opened the first hive, and many bees greeted me, but they had nowhere near completed or even started on their frames in the super. I gently closed the lid without killing one bee and moved onto the second hive. This hive was different when I opened the lid, inside thousands of bees were working, and they were busy making honey on the frames.

I returned to the house and rang my bee supplier, and enquired whether or not I should now by some cut comb frames. The cut comb frame enables me to retrieve some honey without buying an extractor that spins off the frames. This way I can remove the frames and cut out of the honey, wax, pollen, nectar and the odd bee leg. The comb honey is classed as the superior honey to all jars, mainly because you get everything that is suppose to be good for you without all the filtering. The runny honey you get in the jars, has usually been boiled and filtered. I ordered my comb frames and left my bees in peace.

Fortunately I was lucky and managed to drive over to Okehampton within an hour of my phone call, to collect the comb frames and replace them without any mishaps in the super box. My friend Colin stood behind me without any protective clothing, he refuses to wear it, saying my bees are friendly bees and they like him. He handed me the smoker and my hive tool, and between us we replaced the five frames with the comb frames in each hive, ten all together, and walked back up the garden.

I was pleased with myself that I had managed not to kill one single bee in the process. However, five bees who were upset about me removing their drawn out comb, which they had been working very hard on, followed me up the garden. If I had been the bee association man, they would have died, he would have killed them instantly.

But, I let them follow me, four gave up after ten minutes, but one persistent little bugger followed me up to my front door, and came in doors after the frames. I gently shooed it out, not wishing it any harm. It was after all only doing what it was suppose to do, and that was to guard the hive, and I had after all according to the bee stolen part of its home. The bee stayed outside for another four hours, before finally giving up and returning to its hive. I watched it from indoors, flying around buzzing angrily. I knew this bee had only six weeks to live, and who was I to shorten its time on planet earth. So I let it buzz angrily and four hours later it wearily it gave up and returned home. But, it was still alive, my working ethics on bees is to let them live their lives without too much interference from me.

Chapter 7
When Bees Swarm
30th May

Dear Shelagh,

    I was feeling pretty pleased with myself after I last worked on my hive, no bee deaths to report, or bee burials. Of course I am always slightly intimidated when I first lift the hive lid off the hive and thousands upon thousands of bees fly up to greet me. I try to work quickly and carefully so as not to agitated the bees. But, when the sun beats down on my back as I bend over, and the sweat on my face pours down my face, forcing my glasses to slide down my nose and tumble into my suit. There is little I can do about it. I need my glasses to examine the frames, that are crawling with a mass of bees who refuse to move down to their brood box even after a few puffs of smoke.

    My suit for safety reasons is tightly closed with many zips fastening me in, and my hands have tight protective leather gloves on them, so it makes getting my glasses back onto my nose quite difficult, actually impossible, without taking my gloves off first and unzipping my suit, and within seconds bees would have flown in and stung the hell out of me. I usually peer closely at the frames without my glasses that dangle somewhere in my suit, and brush the bees off their frames with a feather, and guess work mainly as to what is going on in their colony.

Then I close the hive lid and replace the top and walk away. Only when I am a safe distance away from the hives, usually by my front door, then I unzip myself and pull off my sweaty gloves, and walk indoors first making sure no bees have followed me inside, and strip out of my sweaty clothes. The smoke lingers in my hair, and I am sure my smell when I am out shopping or meeting my friend John for coffee is one of grass smoke. Not too unpleasant, and could be bottled and sold.

I met up with John for our usual coffee and chat, his father is in hospital not at all well, in fact he does not think he will live for much longer. His father is ninety two and only recently retired as head gardener at a large estate in Newton Abbott.

On my return from my coffee date with John, I walked into the garden, and stopped suddenly because at the bottom of my garden on my neighbours fence post was a black mass of swirling bees, many had now formed a tight ball. I have to admit I was alarmed and horrified, if not a little scared at this sight. I had only ever seen bees like this in books.

Just lately I had realized that my second hive was full of bees, more so than my first hive, which is strange because they arrived at the same time, with the same number of bees inside both hives. But, bees don't read books on bees. Although I did resist the urge to count everyone of them to make sure.

I walked slowly down the garden, and there sure enough were my bees, half the hive had swarmed. Now, this is common at this time of year, when bees expand rapidly and need to separate, and I had been prepared for swarming by reading up on bee books. But, I had not prepared in the Bee Association way that is linked to these books. These books explain in great detail what to do, which is to get inside your hive find your queen cells and destroy them, or separate the bees.

The bees come in three parts, the queen, the workers and the flying bees. Apparently according to my books on bees, if you separate one of these parts from the other two, then a swarm is less likely to happen. But, when reading up on this complicated procedure that does not give any guarantees that it will succeed, I usually close my book and switch on a comedy programme on television instead. I place the book to one side, and try not to think about bees for a while.

The process to stop swarming according to the bee books, was knowing what bees to look for, remove the frames with these bees on them, and then place these frames in another colony or another hive, not sure which, or how.

Either way it requires the bee keeper to spend longer than my usual ten minutes or so with my bees, and to poke inside and around their hive, which could take ages, and end up with thousands of angry, flying, stinging, buggers. I have read and re-read this section on swarming, and still do not understand it.

I had decided to take the other swarm control method, which was to let nature take its course, and let the little buggers fly off with my original queen, who had been marked with a white spot on her back.

I would still have half my bee colony left, although not so much honey, because the swarm always gauge themselves on honey first before leaving. I would hopeful have a new queen that the remainder of the colony had produce, by feeding up one of their cells with royal jelly to prepare ready for their new queen, once the old one leaves. Of course my new queen would not have a white spot on her back, but, I really did not mind, because it saved me the task of killing unnecessary queen cells that the bees had produce, and were quite capable of taking care of themselves. They have done this for over one million years which is how bees produce themselves. They have been working up to this point in their very short lives, to maintain their existence. It is only bee keepers that interfere with their natural lives, mostly because they have prizes for the most produce honey, and with half the colony taking half the honey, bee keepers are not at all happy if they lose this honey. I am not in beekeeping to produce lots of honey, or to win prizes, for me it is the pleasure of watching my bees work, and if any honey is over then I shall be grateful for that.

But, I was faced with thousands of bees on my grumpy neighbour's fence. I rang the store where I have been buying my bee equipment, they have been more helpful then the Devonshire Bee Association lot. 'Do you want another hive?' the man asked me at the other end of the phone from the bee shop. I replied 'no'. I looked at the fence and looked outside, and good fortune was on my side, my neighbour was still at work. She works odd hours and could return at anytime.

'Well leave them then,' the man said, 'they should go within the next couple of hours to find their new home, of course if you did want another bee colony you could catch them in box.' I left the bees on the fence post and had a cup of coffee and rang my friend John who told me his father had just died.

'The hospital has just rang me,' John said. I sipped my coffee and looked anxiously down the bottom of the garden, hoping the bees would disappear before my neighbour returned home. 'What will you do now?' I asked John. There was silence at the end of the phone for a few minutes, 'well,' John said, 'my father asked me before he passed away, to collect a box on top of his wardrobe when he had died.'

I realized I wasn't thinking clearly, and was not at all helpful to my friend John, when I replied whilst staring at my bees hanging off the fence post, 'well your dad won't fit into a box,' I said. Again, a long silence, 'no he won't,' John said, 'the box is for me to take to his solicitor.'

It was not until much later after my bees disappeared and only just before my neighbour return, that I realised what I had said to John. I think he will forgive me.

I was advised to leave the bees alone for a week or so after they had swarmed in order for them to settle down. This advise was from my bee keeping shop, that was so much easier and simpler than the books I read. My swarm control was just to let nature take its course, and after all I do still have, half a colony of bees left, ok, so I won't have as much honey, but I still have friendly bees who have not had their home disturbed, or destroyed. I let them get on with it.

Chapter 8
When Bees Sting

31st May

Dear Shelagh,

    I am leaving my bees alone for the next few weeks. I shall let them settle down and make their new queen. Some beekeepers buy in their queens at about sixty pounds a time. There are even specialist beekeepers who only breed queens for sale. It is quite easy to lose a queen. My first encounter with a fellow beekeeper was at the out-apiary in Exeter. A lady about my age said she had just started to keep bees, and was boasting about the Beekeeping Association's Course she had attended, and had a certificate to prove it. She asked me if I had been on a course, and I shook my head 'no', feeling quite stupid having bought my bees first. But, I did feel somewhat smug and allowed myself a small gloat when the lady followed up her statement about her beekeeping course, with the following sentence, 'well I lost my queen last week, and now my bee colony is not doing so well without its queen.'

I enquired as to how she had lost her queen, and she replied, 'on one of my weekly inspections in the hive. I pulled out a frame to take a look, and my queen must have fallen off. I lost her in the long grass.' Queens don't fly so well, they are too fat to fly, so the queen would not have been able to return to the bee hive. I resisted the urge to reply that her beekeeping course had been successful then. I read somewhere that weekly inspections on your hives, is like pulling up a plant on a weekly bases to check on its roots. It does more harm than good to do this. I also read another article about how beekeepers unwittingly are doing more harm than good on their weekly inspections, because they are subjecting their colony to diseases, for example studies in beekeeping in Africa have found that beekeepers over there, who keep bees in Africa, and who leave their hives alone, have healthier bees than their European counterparts.

During routine colony inspections beekeepers frequently break the natural propolis envelope around their home which acts as a barrier against disease. The British Beekeeping Association promote the use of nasty chemical sprays, used in the colony to protect against some diseases. So the large pharmaceutical companies win via profit making, and the poor bees that have spent millions of years using its own natural defences to fight diseases by building a natural protection around its colony with propolis (a sticky glue stuff made from the sap of trees), loses its fight against disease when this is broken on hive inspection, and in its place the use of unnatural chemicals are used that do more harm then good.

Also artificial selection is costing bees their lives, for example rearing a queen and selling it on for money, again does more harm than good. The bees are good at selecting their own healthy queen, unlike the beekeeper who does not have one million years of practice on 'survival of the fittest', and could and does produce a queen which is often unhealthy, that goes onto producing other unhealthy bees.

Darwin's theory of evolution also included bees, and they have successfully evolved by selecting the fittest species of their kind, unlike us humans, and I was reminded of this as I watched my friend Colin, cutting the grass around the hives, when only a few moments ago, I had specifically told him not to use the lawn mower around the hives because they have only just swarmed, and the bees need to settle down. Swarming makes the bees more alert. The bees have fewer numbers in their colony and therefore, guarding their hive entrance, puts them on high alert, and makes them bad tempered and slightly more aggressive.

I watched Darwin's theory of evolutionary species that got through the gene pool of very few brain cells, wave its arms around in frantic motions, as the angry bees chased him. Colin ran into the shed, I opened the door and listen to the swearing coming from the shed. He was telling the bees to go and multiply off, 'their chasing me Sand,' he yelled as he came running out of the shed. 'There won't leave me alone.' The bees did not leave Colin alone, they buzzed and dive bombed him all afternoon, with one persistent bugger buzzing his head continuously. Four hours later, it gave up. 'I shouldn't have cut the grass around their hives,' Colin said gloomily.

Keeping Bees has put me on alert in a different way. I now look at my environment differently, and always from a bee's point of view, and not from a humans. Man has created a lot of damage to our environment over the centuries, over farming for one, and not taking into account the valuable work that bees do to maintain our food supply, through their pollination. Instead mankind has totally ignored their importance to our crops, and it is only until recently when I started to keep bees that I have started to learn from them.

They are so interesting and unlike any other creature on our planet. Yesterday morning I went dressed ready to inspect my hives. I had a good reason to inspect them. I wanted to make sure they were not overcrowded. I was only going to remove the lid off their hive and take a quick peep inside their super to see if this has been filled with either brood or comb. I also wanted to try and remove their queen excluder to give them more room for making brood and hopefully less likely to swarm. I had read up on this, and apparently this was a much easier way to stop swarming, instead of killing queen cells.

I had my smoker armed and ready, the beekeeper's only natural defence against bees. Smoking keeps the bees down, and the beekeeper can work without too much interference. This I read, but unfortunately for me the bloody bees had not read the books.

My first hive I managed successfully. I removed the lid, checked the frames, most were being drawn out into cells for honey. I lifted the queen excluder off the brood box and replaced the super box on top. Great no squashed or dead bees in that little bit of work. I moved onto the next hive, and attempted to carry out the same procedure. Unfortunately bees came to the top and refused to move down with my puffs of smoke. I quickly replaced the hive lid but in dosing so killed a couple of bees.

I walked back up the garden feeling dreadful, and against my better judgement, and lacking in experience or knowledge on beekeeping, I went to take another look and try and remove the queen excluder, and feeling guilty, remove the dead bees I had killed. Their crushed bodies on the hive is an unpleasant reminder of what I had done to them. I yelled to Colin to pass me the smoker which he did. Colin's job in my beekeeping is to keep the smoker alight, that is all he does an easy task. I lifted off the hive lid and waited for the smoker to be passed to me, but it never came, 'its gone out,' Colin yelled.

I was faced with a beekeeper's worst scenario, an absolute nightmare. and I was too inexperience to know what to do. Suddenly out of the hive poured thousands upon thousands of bees, like oil being poured from an oil can, or even worse like opening the gates to a dam. The bees flowed out, there was no stopping them. I tried desperately to brush them off with my gloves, and use my pathetic feather which was useless against so many bees. Instead in sheer panic I placed the lid down on the hive, and in doing so, squashed a lot more bees, many more than I had done just a few minutes ago. The noise of their deaths will haunt me forever, the breaking of their bodies, and the loud buzzing sound was extremely frightening.

I quickly walked away, with Colin words ringing in my ears, 'Sand you have thousands of bees chasing you.' I looked around, and sure enough bees were covering my protective suit. I tried to stand still but instinct was to run, I brushed them off my arm, but one stung me. I was badly stung.

I waited for a few minutes until all the bees had gone, and removed my suit. My arm had swollen up within seconds. It throbbed and ached. I had been punished by the bee for killing members of its colony, its family, and I accepted my punishment, and waited for the inevitable painful swelling on my arm to appear. Because I do have a bad reaction to bee stings.

I felt dreadful, like the worse beekeeper ever. I rang the National Bee Supply in Okehampton, and in tears explained my predicament. A kindly man at the end of the phone said 'you are not the first or last to do that. We all have to learn.' I listen between sobs, seriously thinking of giving it up. The man at the end of the phone continued, 'think of it like this,' he said, 'you haven't killed an animal or a whole being. Bees are different, they are and live like one entity, you did what you did to save a the whole colony, to stop them all pouring out. Bees are one creature, unlike anything else on planet earth.' His words held some comfort, and I arranged to go and collect the extra super boxes from their store for my hives the following day.

I read later in my bee book, that honey bees unlike the bumble bee and unlike any other bee work and live together, and cannot survive without the colony. Honey bees cannot live alone. They produce as one, and live as one. I wondered if mankind could learn from the honey bee, to live as one entity on earth, and then perhaps the resources could be shared.

Chapter 9
When Bee Stings Hurt
4th June

Dear Shelagh,

     sleeping was not easy, after my last sting when my bees attacked me, for killing so many of them. My arm throbbed all night long, and if I accidental turned over on my arm, the throbbing became more intense. It was also a painful reminder that I was not dealing with docile chickens, or any other livestock. In fact I was dealing with a potentially dangerous entity, that could quite easily attack and kill if I were to lose control of it, and worryingly I have little hands on experience as to what I am doing.

    The other day if I had panicked I could have induced a far worse scenario, because if I had left the hive lid off, angry bees would have spilled out and flown a few feet over the fence, attacking and stinging my neighbours. So, I am thankful that at least I remained calm and placed the lid on the hive, and therefore containing my bees, and allowing them to settle down and adjust to their daily living without my heavy handed interference.

I went to the National Bee supply the day after my incident with my bees, I had lost all confidence in beekeeping, and was going to arrange for them to be sold on. I walked into the shop which is part of a large factory where they make the hives that are shipped all over the country and abroad, and promptly burst into tears. The owner, a very kindly man spent an hour and half with me, teaching me about bees, and showed his concern when I explained that I did not have a bee buddy because I was not happy with the bee buddy from the Devonshire Bee Association, 'he killed so many of my bees,' I sniffed and sobbed.

I left the National Bee Supply armed with my new super to place on top of the other super. This one has cut comb inside, which means when the bees have filled this, then at least I can enjoy some honey. But, to remove the honey is again another matter, because effectively you are stealing the bee's honey and they do get angry about this. There are certain procedures on how to carry out removing honey supers, but I have not read that far yet in my book. I shall be a little nervous about taking the honey frames out of the super when they are full. But, that won't be for sometime yet, and hopefully I should have gained some confidence by then.

The gentleman from the National Bee supply had unbeknown to me, contacted the bee farmer where I had originally purchased my bees from, who is an ex police officer, and has retired and now a bee farmer. The bee farmer phoned me up, and has kindly offered for me to go and stay with him for the day learning hands on how to look after bees. This will be practical experience for me. I have spent many hours pouring over my books, which is my theory, but I do not have the practical experience I really need.

I have arrange to go and spend the day with the bee farmer next Tuesday. I am nervous, the last time I was there I got stung, but I am also excited about watching a professional beekeeper at work, and I hope to build up my own confidence to handle my bees.

After I returned home from the National Bee Supply, I walked nervously down the garden, all dressed up in my beekeeping gear, and with a throbbing arm, and with a much needed lit smoker, bellowing away. I had threatened Colin that he would be strung up if he let the dam thing out again. But, smoke poured out of it, if anything he had overdone it. Still, I cautiously removed the lid off the hive, and smoked the bees with a few puffs, waited until they went down the hive, and placed the super on top. I felt huge relief when I walked away after successfully completing this procedure, without killing or upsetting the bees.

My first hive now has a brood box, where baby bees are made, and honey stores for the bees themselves, plus an extra brood box where I had placed a super on top, but had removed the queen excluder. But, after words of advice from the chap at the National Bee supply, I had replaced the queen excluder back on my new super. This would then keep the queen from laying eggs in this super. Then I can eat this honey.

What I had done apparently, when removing the queen excluder when I should not have done so, was to create a brood and half of baby bees, and expanded my colony. I was informed that because I had left the queen excluder off the first super, then I would end up with cut comb frames, with honey inside, but possibly with baby bees or larva (bee eggs) laid by the queen inside the honeycomb as well, and since I am a vegetarian the thought of eating honey with bits of bees inside, did not appeal to me. It was with this in mind that I went down the route of taking the advice I had been given, and placed the queen excluder on top of my new super.

There is so much debate on this subject, whether or not to put a queen excluder on a super. Some beekeepers argue that putting a queen excluder on top of a super holds back the honey supply with the worker bees refusing to go up into the new super without their queen, which creates a shortage of honey in the first place. Others argue that to leave the queen excluder off your super, you then get baby bees laid in your honey because the queen is able to go through to the upper super and lay eggs inside those frames.

I have gone with placing the queen excluder on top of my second super, therefore, comprise between the two schools of thoughts. Who would have thought that beekeeping could be fraught with so many differing ideas. I naively thought that bees were bees and beekeeping was simple. How wrong I was. If you ask nine beekeepers a question about beekeeping, then you would get nine different answers. I suppose in time you get to learn what works for you. But, at the moment, I am so desperate for any advice, I am soaking up too much information, and getting confused.

To clear my head after placing my second super on my first hive, I went for a walk with the dogs. I have not placed a second super on my second hive yet, because this is the hive that I panicked over and killed so many bees. I am leaving them alone for a week or two, and besides I really cannot face their crushed dead bodies yet.

My dogs enjoy sunny afternoons lying on the small piece of grass enclosed from my chickens, who would go about systematically destroying my garden if it were not chicken proof. My wild flower garden is coming along nicely, created with bees in mind. When I realized I was going to have bees, I asked my friend Colin to create a wild flower section in my garden.

A large square part of my garden was dug up and I bought a packet of wild flower seeds, and patio stones to walk along so as not to walk on the flowers when looking at them.

However, my wild flower garden has a mass of flowers all growing down one end of it, whilst the other section is void of all flowers. It looks as though someone has thrown a packet of seeds on the ground and left them there.

That is exactly what happened. Colin after digging the wild flower garden, walked over to distributed the seeds evenly, only he tripped over a patio stone he had laid just in front of the wild flower garden. The packet fell from his hands and seeds landed in a pile, and they have now grown in a huge bunch at the end of one part of the garden. They are not sprinkled evenly over the area. They are so clumped and bunched together it is a wonder that any flowers can actually grow through. But, some have.

Early this year I purchased a wooden bench near the wild flower section of my garden, with the intention of sitting and watching my bees as they collected pollen from the flowers. Only my bees miss my flowers, and head straight to my neighbours beautiful pink bush that hangs slightly over my fence. My bees congregate on that bush, hundreds of them, wiping the pollen from the pink flowers and placing them in a sack in the back of their legs. They are fascinating creatures to watch at work, and do not mind me peering up close at them with my glasses on. They fly around me, working away, not at all bothering me. I feel privilege to watch them working. I am still not sure how my neighbour feels about my bee invasion on her plants and bushes.

The scout bees will fly back to their hive and do the waggle dance alerting the bees inside to where the pollen is. The bees do this by dancing in a circle. Their dance is their language to each other. The bees use the sun to navigate because they can see polarized light they know its position even when it is not directly visible to us. The dances performed in the hive use the vertical to indicate the position of the sun outside the hive and what is truly amazing, the angle of the dance alters to take into account the sun's movement during the day.

The length of the waggle indicates the distance to the food source. The longer the waggle time the further away the food. Inside the hive, their direction towards the sun is vertically upwards. So if the direction of the food source is towards the sun, the dancer faces straight up the face of the comb when performing the waggle. From how vigorous the dance, is how rich the food source. The bee's ability to communicate with each other is quite amazing, but so to are the bee's ability to be aware of the earth's magnate field.

My bees have taught me a lot about my morning walks with my dogs, for example the word 'honeydew' is related to the honey bee. Aphids feed on plant sap but reject the sugar they suck in. The sugar falls on the leaves and is semi diluted by dew. This is collected by bees and other insects. My knowledge about honeydew has given me a different way of looking at plants on my early morning walks. My dogs when walking through the long grasses have often had honeydew on their noses, now I see it as nature way of creating sugar for bees to make honey. How finely tuned nature is with her insect and bug life. I suppose with our life as well if we let nature into it.

Chapter 10

Dear Shelagh

5th June

Dear Shelagh,

The Quicks who make cheese and have fields opposite me and have hundreds of cows milling around in their fields. My bee book Bee Quest has made me aware of what happens if we leave nature alone and let it return to its natural state. At Knepp estate the wildlife has been left to its own defences, and even cows are able to roam freely. Unlike the Quicks cows who are bundled up together in small fields, and just a product for their cheese making machines, at Knepp, their cows are able to take of themselves.

These once domestic breeds who have lived in captivity for hundreds of generations, still retain their natural instincts. The cows naturally form themselves into herds of a dozen or so, led by a dominant female. If the group becomes too big, it divides into two and they go their separate ways. Which is remarkable, given I have seen the over populated and densely filled Quicks's fields full of cows, with no thought to the welfare of their animals. I refuse to eat their cheese on principle. It is a heart rendering noise to hear the mother cow crying, when her young are forcible removed from her so young, in order for the cows to produce the milk for their cheese.

Cows on the Knepp estate are allowed to give birth freely, and when the cow is about to give birth she will leave the herd and go into the dense undergrowth in the woods. There she leaves the calf, returning to the herd for much of the day, but popping back to suckle the calf at intervals. This might seem strange, but this strategy for the new born calf who is helpless and leaving it alone and unprotected in the woods, works. Deer also do the same thing. This is because tucking the calf out of sight in the woods, is far safer then having it out in the open where it would be very obvious to a wolf pack to stalk the heard and worry them out of the way, and therefore able to make the herd leave the calf all alone and a potentially an easy meal. This way, the calf is not with the herd and is out of harms way.

It is reassuring to learn, that animals which have been used and domesticated by man such as cows can and still do retain their natural ways and instincts. I wonder if we too can retain our natural instincts that have become lost through being locked into our mobile world and other devices.

Having bees does make me aware of my own environment, much more so than before. When I walk into

Crediton past an old abandoned industrial site, which is close to the golf course and on my walk with my dogs, I now take a few minutes longer, to stand and look at the site with more interest, with my own bees in mind. In industrial sites, there are fewer nutrients in the soil, away from the over use of artificial fertilisers that cause the soil to become too high in nitrate. In such soils with high nutrients a profusion of nettles, docks and cow parsley sprout like triffids, these are the few species that thrive in high nitrate soils.

I have walked past the hedgerow and seen these sprouting plant species, which are often next to the fields in the countryside. But, the abandoned industrial site, that I took time to notice, had a different plant species. Here without the harsh artificial fertilisers and with fewer nutrients in the soil, there are many different plant species sprouting through cracked tarmac. As though nature is beginning to take over man's efforts to build over the land. Here in amongst the chipped and discarded building material, are different types of flowers, not your usual triffids, but delicate flowers, such as cowslips and what looks like orchids, and when I looked closely at these flowers I can see a wide selection of insects and bees.

It is lovely to see nature reclaiming its land, and producing an abundance of wild delicate flowers for the fine balance of insects to survive. But, recently I noticed a large noticed over the rusty, iron gate, a planning application for a new housing estate has been granted permission. This little oasis for plants, insects and bugs, will have to move on or be destroyed. Mankind appears to quite happily bulldozer over such delicate areas of natural beauty, in the name of development. Quite ironic really, the word development, when really it means destroying.

I am also more in tune with the weather than I was before I had bees. Previously when I looked out of the window and saw dark rain clouds on the horizon, it would mean a hurried walk for myself and my dogs, and nothing more. Wet weather is not something my standard Poodle likes, in fact she hates it, and refuses to leave the house if it is raining heavy outside. She has been known to push her paws hard into the floor, and refuses to budge holding herself until it stops raining to go to the toilet. Cold weather was not too bad, the dogs and I still enjoyed our walks, and even if it was windy we still went walking. I did not take much notice of the weather.

However, since my bees have been on the scene, weather patterns take on a whole new meaning to mean. Bees do not like flying if it is too windy, they find it hard work, and it can quickly exhaust them, and if there is not enough honey supplies for them in their hive, they can quickly die of starvation. In order to prevent this, the beekeeper must ensure there is enough honey before removing any for his or her own use, or adding a sugar and water solution to their feed.

The bees do not like the cold, and will stay in the hive huddled around their queen to keep her warm, the outside bees around their queen often die of cold first. If it is too hot, the bees do the same thing, only they use their wings to act as a fanning motion to cool the hive down. Too much damp in the hive is not good for bees, so maintaining a damp prove hive is very important, there has to be sufficient ventilation. The bees do not like the rain, and this hampers their supply of nectar and pollen to create their food. The bees can be grumpy on cold, wet weather conditions, and is advised to leave them well alone. The same for cold and windy conditions.

The best honey flow conditions are hot weather but not necessarily sunny, high humidity and heat which enhances the nectar production in flowers, that is good for the bees. Very hot weather is not good, it dries up the sap in the plant so therefore no nectar for the bees. All this information I only learnt since keeping bees, before this, I was only concerned with wet weather, and wondering if my washing could be pegged out on the line, or could I get my Poodle out of the door. Now, the bees down the bottom of my garden that make honey, depend on certain weather conditions, in order to survive, and have made me much more aware of our climate and seasons in Devon.

I have recently purchased a second bird bath. It was only after reading one of my books on beekeeping that I realized that bees require water close on hand, well at least twenty yards away from their hives, (or was it meters I can't remember which).

The river across the road from where the bee hives are situated, would have been their main source of water, but they would have had to fly some distance to it, and if the weather is not good, this then would not be an ideal situation for them. So, to keep the bees happy, I was advised by my bee farmer to have a water supply close to the hives, but not too close. This would then make sure the bees did not have to fly to far from their hives and therefore, not exhaust themselves to much. Apparently the key to a happy bee, and lots of honey, is to make sure the bees are not flying too far, even for their pollen and nectar. Some bees will travel up to five miles away for food.

I purchased one bird bath, and placed a few stones in and around the edges of it, to give the bees support so they do not fly straight into it and drown. In the wild bees will find a shallow pebble surface to land on and drink between the pebbles or gravel.

This appeared to work, and was going well. I would often watch about twenty bees on the stones in my bird bath drinking away. But, not long after installing the bird bath, so too came the rooks, crows and black birds. The birds, not the pretty small kind, for those tend to fly into my neighbour's gardens. Oh no, I have the big crows, and rooks in my garden, feasting on my chicken food. The crows and rooks love their new birdbath, and being large birds, have taken over it, splashing, bathing, and drinking from it. So my poor bees have been crowded out.

In order to rectify this problem, I had to purchase another bird bath, and install this next to the original bird bath. This bird bath is larger and wider, so the birds and bees if necessary can share the bird bath with plenty of room for all.

It has not worked out like this. Both, birds and bees fight for the much smaller original bird bath, and I have seen both birds and bees drinking from the same bird bath, totally ignoring the new one. My two old cats are sixteen and fifteen years old, and just love sitting under the chicken hutch watching the birds on the bird bath. The cats make no attempt to chase the birds. I guess the old cats bones are just not up to the chase any more. So the birds walk beneath the cats noses, and the cats swish their tails from time to time, neither taking much notice of the other. Bees, birds, chickens and cats all enjoy warm sunny days in my garden in very close proximity to each other.

Chapter 11

Bee Venom is it Good for You?

8th June

Dear Shelagh,

    I am convinced that my knee is much better since I have been stung three times by my bees. Before my stings, I had been suffering with a painful knee joint, that made walking quite difficult at times, in fact I would limp down the garden and back. But, since my bee stings, my knee is less painful. I wonder if there was something in what I read the other day, that bee stings help with arthritis, such a coincidence if it were not true. I often had sleepless nights tossing and turning with the pain and throbbing ache in my knee keeping me awake. But, now, touch wood, my knees is less painful, and I finally sleep at night and what is more the best sleep I have had for sometime.

    I went to the Bee shop yesterday, my helpful shop, the one and only bee people that have given me good advice on keeping bees. I had to buy another super for my second hive. I had already last week bought my second supper and placed this on my first hive, which now gives me a brood box and a super full of brood and honey (I hope, I have not checked this out by smoking the buggers and peering into their hives), and a recently purchased super on top full of cut comb which if and when this is filled by my bees, should give me some honey.

I have now bought the second super for my second hive, and without too much trouble, with the smoker going full pelt, today I manage to place the second super on top of this hive. Both my hives are now the same height with the same number of boxes inside. There is now a queen excluder between the first super and the recently purchased new super (second super) which keeps the queen out from laying eggs and brood into my honey super. I was not keen on eating baby bees in the cells, mixed in the cut comb.

Colin watched me quite close up when I worked on my bees, whilst I placed the second super on top of the second hive, 'they did not sting you this time San,' he yelled at me, quite helpfully. But, unfortunately this did give Colin confidence to yet again go down to my bees and cut the grass around their hives. I cannot remember how many times I have told him not to get too close to the hives when cutting the grass.

Early this morning it was windy and cloudy and the sky looked gloomy, full of potential storm clouds hurrying past. It was also cold for June, in fact I went back indoors and put my warm coat on. I cleaned the chickens and fed them, then leaving Colin to potter around the garden, because he loves pottering, I made a cup of coffee for both of us. Whilst waiting for the kettle to boil, I looked down the garden.

There was a very funny occurrence or disturbance at the bottom of the garden, in fact I did chuckle to myself out loud, as Colin ran back up the garden peeling his clothes off whilst running. He hurriedly removed his coat, slung this to the ground, bent over and furiously brushed his hair with his hands, then removed his cardigan and threw this down, and again beat himself on his chest with his fists, then his tee-shirt was also quickly removed and this too was thrown down. Colin then ran wildly around the garden, naked from the top, shouting 'bloody bees'.

I enquired as to what was wrong, and was informed amongst erratic beatings and frantic arm waving, that he was being chased by about fifty bees, give or take a bee. 'Why?' I asked, and was told by Colin that there were no bees outside the hives, and the grass outside the entrance to the hives needed cutting. So, Colin went into the hive areas, checked to see that there were no bees outside, and proceeded to kneel by their hive entrance and with sheers in his hands cut away. He was only minutes, perhaps less when a swarm of about fifty bees or so decided that their colony was being invaded and sent out the attack squad.

The bees buzzed around Colin for an hour, and how he was not stung by one bee is completely beyond me. I go to the trouble of wearing protective clothing, and yet the bees still manage to get through and sting me. But, Colin who torments the buggers by annoying the hell out of them, and kneels at their hive entrance, which is a huge no, no in all my beekeeping books, does not get stung once. It does seem rather unfair.

However, it was a sometime before Colin could remove his items of clothing, because the bees had descended on these, obviously thinking this was the nearest thing they could get to their potential enemy at their door. Colin informed me later that he would not be doing that again. But, I am not so sure. I have written about Colin before in my letters to you, and Colin did and has done the same thing again. He unfortunately does not learn, and thinks if the bees are not out of their hive then all is safe. But the bees have guards at their entrance to stop robbers stealing their honey. They are not at all stupid, and can smell and sense when there is an intruder near their hives.

The best thing to do was to leave the bees well alone until they calmed down, and were reassured that their colony was not under threat or attack. I decided to not go near them for a few days.

Chapter 12
A very Swollen Colin

20 June

Dear Shelagh,

I was shocked when I called around Colin's the morning after his attack from my bees. Colin had insisted that he had not been stung by the bees, in fact proud of it, but by the sight of his face when he greeted me at his front door, things said otherwise.

It was hard for me not to laugh when I was confronted with what can only be described as something that looked very similar or worse even, a Quasimodo look alike. Colin's face hung limply down the left side, ballooned out, so much so that his left eye was not visible, and his cheeks were bright red and swollen. If I had not known what had happened to him, I would have thought he had been badly beaten during the night and that his flat had been broken into, and his assailants handing out a terrible beating to him.

He had been beaten though, but by my honeybees, the ladies of the colony, and what a good thrashing they had given him. Colin raised his right arm to stoke his face, this too was swollen, he could not even form his hand into a fist, his fingers thick like fat, pork, sausages. I made Colin a cup of tea, and watched as he struggled to drink it, unable to lift the cup to his swollen lips and mouth.

'Did the bees get you then?' I asked, concerned but also desperately trying not to sardonically laugh or smile at him, whilst the swollen mess sat in front of me. 'I think so,' Colin said, 'shan't be going down there again for a while,' he muttered more to himself then to me, and I couldn't hear properly due to the heavy lisping through thick lips.

The most embarrassing situation was at the shops. Colin followed me into Tesco to buy a few items. But, I quickly made him return to the car and sit in it until I came back with his shopping for him. It was the way the parents gathered their children close to themselves, and covered their children's eyes, as they looked on in horror as Colin shuffled past them, bedraggled, limping, swinging his thick fingers and swollen arm, whilst trying to give some sort of smile through his swollen lips and face, showing instead a Frankenstein Monster look, his one good eye feverishly trying to see, whilst the other eye completely gone, he instead looked down at the horrified children, who cowered in fear. 'Send him away,' I heard one child cry to its parents.

'You need to get some antihistamine tablets inside you,' I said to Colin, 'and quickly.'

It took a few days for Colin's swelling to go down, and at one point I seriously thought he should see a doctor, but Colin refused, insisting it was nothing more than a bee sting. But, to me it looked like at least ten or more stings. The girls had got him, and when I looked around at the area where Colin had been cutting in front of the hives, there were a few dead bees lying around, hard evidence that in fact he had been stung more than once.

The grassy area around the bee hives was growing fast, and one of the entrances to the left hive, was nearly closed in with nettles. The area required urgently clearing. I suggested to Colin that he get the garden shears out from the shed, and let me try and cut around the hive entrances whilst I wore my bee protective suit.

Colin agreed and thought this and excellent idea. By now his face was back to normal, and his hand and arm was less swollen.

Heather my daughter, asked me to look after the girls for a few hours whilst Rob her husband, and herself, went off for lunch. The morning was humid, and the bees were out in full force on my wild flower garden. I suggested to Colin that I would cut around the hives with my bee protective clothing on when I returned from my babysitting duties, and when the evening air was less humid, and more bees hopefully inside their hive.

Other beekeepers suggest working on the hives during the middle of the day when the forging bees are out, so less bees in the colony, and in the hive. But, so far this has failed to work. For me, there are always thousands of bees flying around, no matter what time of day, whether early morning or late evening. There never appears to be a good time to work on the hives, and only using smoke and good common sense appears to keep stings away whilst working on bee hives.

I returned from my babysitting duties shocked to see a Colin running up the garden, wearing a full protective bee suit. My bee suit. He was fleeing from something, but from that distance I could not see what it was. It was only when Colin started to frantically rip apart the bee protective suit that I realised that he was being chased once again.

'Two are in the suit up by my face,' Colin screamed at me. 'The rest are on my arms,' he shouted. I watched horrified as Colin tugged away frantically at the many zips on the suit. It was a race between him removing the suit quickly, before a very frustrated bee flying around dangerously close to his face in the suit got fed up and stung him.

'Keep still,' I yelled to Colin, 'if you keep still the bee won't be frightened or alarm and will gently fly out of the suit.' Colin ignored my advice, perhaps understandably so, because I wondered if I would be able to keep perfectly still whilst a very angry bee flew inches from my nose, with its sting at the ready, and no matter how many times you get stung, it is that waiting for the pain to strike you, and the steady realisation that sooner rather than later you will be hurting, and then itching and then swelling badly.

Colin pulled and tugged at the suit whilst the bees, a good few of them, buzzed his head and arms, the suit was finally removed and thrown to the ground. 'What happened?' I asked Colin, who stood breathless in front of me, shaking and swiping away at his arms. 'Well I used the lawnmower in front of the bee hives to cut the grass, and I thought wearing the suit would keep them away from me. But, the bees soon came out, and chased me. Its, just no good San,' Colin moaned, 'there is no way to cut the grass in front of the hives.'

Once again the following morning, as though time had repeated itself, like ground hog day, Colin appeared at his front door to his flat, this time his right eye was swollen, and his arms both of them swollen, with thick sausages hanging limply from the ends of his hands. 'They got me good and proper this time,' Colin said, like a solider returning from the front line of duty. I handed the tablets over, and hid Colin for a few days, thinking that by now, I would be called into questioning by the police, perhaps reported for abusing poor old Colin, when in fact, he had been once again been beaten by my female bees. It was them that had abused poor Colin.

Four persistent bees stayed around the top half of the garden for the next four days. Even, unusually when I went to fill the bird bath with water for the bees to drink from, I too got buzzed. I also got buzzed by one bee when I hung my washing out on the line, which was a good few meters from their hives. This had never happened before. I had not been buzzed by any of my bees so close to the house. It was as though this second incident so close to the first was enough for my bees, and they had taken up guarding the area further away from their hives.

Before the grass cutting incident I was able to stand close to their hives without my bee protective suit on, and watch the bees coming and going in and out of their hives. But, the following days after the grass cutting incident, I could only get as far as the back door and even then there was still one bee waiting, that continuously buzzed me. It was astonishing to watch such behaviour. How protective the bees are with their colonies, and what excellent guards they place in front of their hives. It is no wonder how they have manage to survive for millions of years.

And, bees seem to remember, they do not forget easily. The bees station guards further away from their hives. Before the grass cutting incident only a few bee guards were present, these just inside their hive. After the grass cutting incidents the bees stationed their guards by the bird bath further away from their hives, and further still by my washing line, where I was buzzed by a curious bee, when hanging my washing out. The bee did not sting me, just flew close to my body and circled me a few times.

Perhaps what was most astonishing was the single solitary bee who kept guard by my back door, one hundred yards away from their hive, and my entrance into the garden. It flew around my back door, watching and diving at me, but after a week things returned to normal, and the bees allowed to watch them working in and out of their hives, without my bee protective suit on.

I googled how to cut grass in front of the bee hives later that evening, and learnt that the first and most important step is to cover the entrance to the hives with foam to stop the bees coming out. And, the second important step was to use smoke at the entrance to their hive. Alternatively it has been said, that using a strimmer rather than a mower could be better for the bees, but if able to, close the hive entrance with foam, and still smoke the bees.

Apparently the mower frightens the bees with its loud noise and vibration, they probably think it is a storm brewing and dislike thunder and storms, and get very volatile. After Colin's swelling eased, I suggested perhaps blocking the entrance to the bee hives before cutting the grass in front of them. Doing it this way, would ensure that the bees could not come out and attack. I also explained to Colin that a strimmer would be a better way to clear and cut in front of hives, less noise, and also no vibration.

A few days later after a coffee and cake with my friend John in Crediton, I returned home to find a very happy

Colin. He had beaten the bees, and proudly showed me how he had cut the grass in front of the bee hives. 'The strimmer works,' Colin said, smiling. 'They do not mind the strimmer at all, no need to block the entrance or wear the suit,' Colin said.

Once again, Colin had taken a chance with my bees, but at least this time he had not got stung. So after some very painful experiences for Colin, and some very painful lessons learnt, he now only uses the strimmer to cut the grass in front of the bee hives. But, I do wish he would wait for me before cutting in front of the hives. With such dangerous creatures, it is not wise to do such things on your own, accidents are waiting to happen. Or in Colin's case, bees are waiting and watching him.

Chapter 13

Learning to be a Proper Beekeeper

22nd June

Dear Shelagh,

  I had a phone call the other evening from the bee farmer at Holsworthy, it was late in the evening just after nine pm. I am usually in bed just after nine in the evenings, because I am always up at five in the morning especially with the light mornings. I like to get up early to let the chickens out, because they are always eager come out of their coup. They then fly down to the bottom of the garden to grab the early morning worms, and then I always take a peak at my bee hives, just checking things are ok and not a cluster of dead bees in front of the hive entrance which is not good. I then clean the bird baths out, ready to fill up with fresh water for both the bees and the birds, and the occasional chicken and cat that also like to drink from the bird baths. After all this, I then take the dogs for a long walk.

So, I was quite tired when my phone rang in the evening, in fact it made me jump. The bee farmer at the end of the phone said his name, but I missed that, so I still do not know his first name, which is embarrassing, and I always try to talk to him without mentioning his name. The bee farmer invited me over to work with him on his hives. He has over forty two hives dotted all over the place, in people's gardens, in fields, and on top of hills.

I was suppose to have gone over to work with him earlier this month on his hives, but something else came up, I think it was when I looked after Phoebe for the day. I arranged a date and time to travel to Holsworthy, which is about an hours drive from my home. I planned to visit Holsworthy before my trip to Aldershot.

It was on the Friday, a few days after my planned trip to Holsworthy that I would be travelling to Aldershot to stay at Carl's house whilst he went over to Cyprus for a brief holiday. Carl is similar to me, he also loves his animals, and has two rescue dogs, one of the dogs came from Cyprus, a rescue cat, and a hamster. There are also three foxes that live down the bottom of his garden which he feeds daily, and has made a lovely den for them both. At least there, they are tucked safely out of his harms way and not hunted, the foxes live quite a peaceful life.

The foxes wander around the army golf course, the golfers never mind, and play around the foxes. I stood and watched them on my last visit, surprised at how the golfers and foxes muddled along together, each one not taking a bit of notice of the other. So different to where I live in Devon, where foxes are hunted for pleasure.

I removed all my protective clothing, my gloves and large wellington boots from the shed at the bottom of my garden, and placed everything in the back of the car. I would take a slow drive across Devon, virtually coast to coast, the east coast of Devon where I lives to the west coast near Bude. It is a beautiful drive with some stunning Devonshire views across the hills, taking in Exmoor and Dartmoor, Holsworthy is situated between the two moors. Only the drive that day was taking exceptionally long. I had forgotten it was market day, and all the slow moving transport of cattle seem to take for ever. I had arranged to be at the bee farmers for ten am, but stuck behind a battered old car and an equally battered old trailer, carrying two sheep, which slowed down to ten miles an hour on hills and bends, the journey seem to go on for ever.

I was panicking because I knew the bee farmer had to travel some distance to his own hives, and he could not hang about waiting for me at his home. My blood pressure increased as did my anxiety levels due to the farmer in front of me, who hardly once pressed his foot on the accelerator. There is no place to overtake on these road, patience is the only thing you can have, as you sit behind such slow moving traffic.

Eventually nearly two hours later I rolled up to the bee farmer's cottage, after I had taken a wrong turning myself. I found the bee farmer still eating his breakfast and would not be ready himself for a while.

The sun was hotting up fast, I knew it was going to be a hot humid day, and standing around in a full bee protective suit, with my jumper and thick trousers on underneath, meant that some serious sweating was going to take place. I had learnt from bitter and painful experience that wearing thin items of clothing underneath a bee suit, meant that stings would take place, and not a good idea. The choice was really get stung but stay cool and not sweat, or sweat and perhaps have a good chance of avoiding being stung.

The bee farmer arrived at his car, wearing only a thin tee-shirt underneath his bee suit, he was obviously going for the might get stung, but not sweat choice. The journey to his apiary was one that I would not easily forget. I was swung around corners at such a rate of knots, that my head jarred back and forwards, I felt car sick. I was already hot, sweating, and for good measure feeling dreadfully sick by the time we arrived at his apiary.

I sort of staggered out of the car, my wellington boots sticking to my heavy woollen socks, my thick jumper stuck to me underneath my bee protective suit, and my face poured sweat so much that I was unable to see.

It was not a good start, and got progressively worse when I tripped over a log unable to see because of the sweat in my eyes, and fell down a hole. 'Oh watch that log, and ok watch that hole,' the bee farmer said, as I fell into a pile of nettles.

The four bee hives where situated in someone's garden, tucked away at the bottom, and looking at the brambles and overgrown weeds surrounding them, it appeared to me that someone else did not enjoy cutting around their bee hives.

The bee farmer set to work. He removed the lid off the first hive, and slowly cut away the wax from the queen excluder, and then lifted each frame out that was covered in bees. He told me that he checks on them once again. I could see the small, white, grubs inside the wax in the middle of the frames, and on the outside of the frames, this was surrounded by honey. The queen had been busy laying eggs, and the frames were a perfect example of a bee colony working as it should.

The second hive had more queen cells which meant the colony was ready to swarm. The beekeeper proceeded to scrape away the queen cells, and located the old queen, which was a good sign that it had not already swarmed. The colony he said was overcrowded and needed an extra super on top, to try and stop it from swarming by giving it more room to expand. I offered to walk back to the car and collect the super for him.

The sun beat down on me, and my head hurt, I think from dehydration. I was beginning to regret not bringing a cold drink with me. I had not realized that it was going to take quite a bit of time to look through four hives. I only spend the minimum time on my hives, not wishing to upset the colony by lifting the frames out from the brood box, where the queen is busy. I have never done this on my hives. I am also worried that I might lose my queen on the grass if I were not careful. Something that the bee farmer was now concerned about, as he desperately searched for the queen from the third hive. He had hung the frames over the hives, but a lot of bees had fallen off.

I asked what happened if the colony was not going well, and was told that if the queen was not present, then a new queen would have to be added to the colony. He told me this does not always work, as the worker bees might not accept the new queen and kill her. Therefore you are back to square one.

The third hive was full of drone cells, but no queen, again not a good colony. The bee farmer scrapped away some of the drone cells, leaving some in place on the frame, but the queen was not to be found. The fourth hive was full of bees in a polystyrene hive, (plastic) which is not ideal. Wood hives are better because they allow the colony to breath. The fourth hive, was going to be split, making extra colonies, or a couple of frames from this hive was going to be placed inside a weak colony to boast them up.

It all sounded so technical, so much interference from man, and still there were no guarantees that whatever, the bee farmer did, might not work. My beekeeping was so different, less interference with the bees, and occasionally I wander down the garden to take a peak outside their hives. But, I see no need to open up their hives and scrape, and dig away either the wax, queen or drone cells. Surely the bees are quite capably of managing their own colonies. I feel they have done so for many millions of years, and would know better than me what was best for them.

I left the bee farmer four hours later, the work on the hives same to take forever. I felt sorry for the bees, as each frame was removed and examined, turned this way and that, they were at one point roughly shaken from their frame into the hive with the reminder of bees being roughly brushed off. They came flying back out, angry as hell. I took a few steps back at this point, not wishing to get stung, and felt the bees had every right to sting the bee farmer.

As I drove away, I asked myself over and over again, what was it with beekeepers that insist on meddling with their hives, and the bees? For what purpose? It made no sense to me. I felt I had been watching some intensive farming, whereby man steps in and takes over from nature, because we are in a hurry to produce honey, and do not let nature take it own course.

I felt comfortable in my own knowledge that I was not an experience beekeeper, but what I had witness so far from the so called experience beekeepers was meddling, and unnecessary interfering in bee hives, just to justify their hobby, or to produce honey on a large scale, or perhaps even, warranting the cost of expensive gadgets for beekeeping. There is an expensive bee brush you can buy, but I just use a feather I found lying in the garden. It appears to do the job just as well.

I was quite happy to let my bees get on with it, and if they do produce an extra bit of honey for me, then that is a bonus.

Chapter 14
At the Hive Entrance

1st July

Dear Shelagh,

  I am staying at my son's house in Aldershot taking care of his animals. The bees are being left to their own devices whilst I am away. Colin is taking a peak now and again at them. He stands to the side of their hives and watches them flying in and out for me. Colin has told me, so far the hive on the right is taking in lots of pollen, and the bees have got white pollen on their legs, probably from the blackberry bushes. There are lots of blackberry bushes along the railway line across the road from me.

  The direction the bees fly in changes with the different flowers in season. This is so interesting to watch. When the bees first arrived at my home late May, they flew in the direction across my neighbours garden to the left of me and into the large field of rape seed oil. They were gathering the pollen and nectar from the yellow rape seed oil flowers. I watched the bees bring in yellow pollen sacks came in on their legs back to their hives.

Three weeks later after the rape seed had finished flowering, the bees changed their flight direction, and flew in a straight line to the bean field, just behind my home. Their direction was in a straight line down my garden to their bee hives, between my house and my neighbours home. It was at times like watching the busy M25, with so much bee traffic.

After the white bean flowers finished, the bees changed their direction once more, and this time flew in all direction. I suppose they were looking for any wild flowers they could find, with pollen, even landing on my own small patch of wild flowers. The bees were lucky to find that some of my fruit trees had late blossom on the trees, and I found one or two bees enjoying the nectar on those.

There is known as a June gap in the bee world, and in some areas, when the spring flowers have finished, and the next flowering season does not start until late in the summer months, the bees can starve if there is not enough honey in their hives. If some beekeepers remove this honey, they should replace it with sugar and water that has been boiled and cooled as a food substitute for their own honey. But in my area, because of the many fields of oil seed rape and the bean flowers, my bees have a continuous source of pollen and nectar. Perhaps in my second year of beekeeping I might be lucky enough and get some honey.

Since I have been away, my friend Colin said the bees have once again changed their flight direction, and headed over the bottom of my garden towards the railway line. It is over there along the railway track that they will find an abundance of blackberries, or little white blackberry flowers. I am not sure what the bees will find in the way of nectar and pollen in late autumn.

When I rang Colin the other morning, he said my bees are returning to their hives with white pollen on their legs, collecting this from the blackberries. It is in a way a shame, that I cannot taste their honey, because I am sure the delicate flavour from the white blackberry and wild flowers would produce a delicately, scented, delicious honey, and all natural, and importantly not a forced or mass produced honey, unlike the bee farmers.

When I was on my way out the other morning with Carl's dog for a walk, I noticed for the first time since arriving here in Aldershot, a bee, and what's more it was a honey bee. I would now be able to recognised those anywhere. She was flying around the blackberry bushes on the white flowers. I only saw the one bee, and given this is an army town, it must have been a wild honey bee, with its nest no further than three miles away.

Since beekeeping I am always on the look out for bees, and this is my first honey bee find since arriving in the town of Aldershot. I have spotted the odd bumble bee or two, but not nearly as many as I have seen in my garden or around in the hedges in Devon.

The bumble bee I spotted was along the Basingstoke canal, and the honey bee was just off the main dual carriageway into Farnham and Aldershot.

I found a book on line yesterday, called 'At the Hive Entrance'. I was googling or searching for 'bees coming in with green pollen on their legs'. Colin rang me the other evening from Devon, and said that my bees had green pollen on their legs. Instead of getting my answer to why my bees have green legs, I found by chance this book all about observing from the hive entrance.

It was written in the fifties by a German beekeeper. I only managed to read a couple of chapters online for free, but what I did read was very interesting. The author H. Storch, wrote that it was not necessary to open the hives up to observe what the bees were up to, all this could be done by sitting and watching the entrance to their hives, and also listening to the tone of the bees inside the hives. It appears to be a very interesting book, and when I return to Devon I shall invest in a copy of it.

Chapter 15

Returning to Boarding School, a Horrid Place

8th July

Dear Shelagh,

 I have finally returned to Devon, and after nearly two weeks away, I am relieved to be back home. I found myself at a lost as to what to do after my friend John left Aldershot. He had spent a week in his Day's Inn, a motorway service hotel, which was cheap, grubby, and bleak, but to John these places are the height of luxury.

 John joined me over at Aldershot for the last week I was staying at Carl's house. John did not stay at Carl's home because his dog hates cats, and Carl has a cat. We manage to complete nine walks for his walking book, 'Meandering Through Hampshire'. It was by chance, that I realized on our last walk, that we were only two miles from my old boarding school, 'Hillsea College', and I managed to persuade John to drive me there to take a look around.

It felt so strange driving up the driveway to the Georgian building, now turned into a smart four star hotel, with posh furnishing, highly, polished, wooden floor, and stranger still to see the spot, now vacant, where the dreaded large, grandfather, clock stood. That punishment clock, whereby, naughty children would stand underneath it, waiting for their punishment, to be dealt out either by caning, slipper or missed supper, missed morning trip to Basingstoke, or the one only treat of the week, missing the black and white film in the large hall.

All my memories came flooding back, especially when I took a walk up the stairs, and to the dormitories. I was very quiet when I returned to John's car, the two dogs sat in the back, and Teigan my old thirteen Standard Poodle licked my face. John spent the rest of the drive back to Aldershot, talking about a pair of walking boots he had had for over two years, and about their condition, and where he had bought them from, how much he paid for them, how he looked after them, and so on. John spent an hour talking about his pair of walking boots, a subject I found hard to even feign any interest whatsoever, even John noticed my quietness when he turned around to the dogs and said, 'she is isn't listening,' of course referring to me, and then backed this statement up by saying, 'rude isn't she?'

Of course my thoughts were else where, some fifty years ago, when I was a young girl living in a place I hated, with just you as the boy's matron, risking your job to show me some warmth from another human being, offering me cocoa in your small room, in the early hours of the mornings.

So, John returned to Devon, and I spent the Monday alone, again lost in my thoughts about my school, but also thinking about my son's return from Dubai in the early hours of the morning. Chris was arriving at Heathrow airport at six thirty in the morning. I would have to leave about five thirty to arrive in time myself, so an early night was on the cards for me.

I soon fell asleep, but was rudely woken up when my mobile phone went off, it was Chris who said his plane had been delayed. My phone rang every hour for his three hour delay, so sleep was useless. Finally at five am his time, he said he was boarding, which meant me arriving at Heathrow around nine thirty am instead of six am.

I was shattered when my alarm went off, I think I only had about two hours sleep all night, and set off in a daze to collect Chris. The plan was to then spend a few days at Carl's with Chris, and he would returned to Essex on the Friday, and I would drive back to Devon on Wednesday morning.

But, our plans went all to pot, when Chris said he was no longer going to Essex. I then put some sort of plan B into place. Chris and I would drive back to Devon at eleven o'clock that evening, after Carl returned from Cyprus, arriving in Devon at one thirty, only a two and half hour drive back along the A303, it would be quiet that time of night. I had assured Chris that it would be easy and a relaxing drive.

Eleven o'clock came and went, both Chris and I sat on the sofa yawning, finding it difficult to keep our eyes open, even though both of us had a power nap earlier that evening. My mobile phone rang, and Carl said they were late arriving in the UK from Cyprus and would not be home until gone twelve, which would have been too late for me to return to Devon. Chris only had until three am Friday morning in Devon, before returning to Essex, so he was eager to get back and make the most of his short stay.

I arranged with Carl to leave his house unlock, and both Chris and I left for our drive back to Devon. The air was humid, still, and sticky, but the roads were clear, and it was not long before I arrived at the beginning of the M3, and only twenty miles later I would join the A303 and sail down the road to Devon, a lovely easy journey.

But, only a short way down the A303 I came to a sign that read, 'A303 CLOSED'. I spent the next hour wrestling with my sat-nav which wanted to keep returning me to the A303, but no matter how far I travelled through the small, narrow, country, lanes, I would return to the A303 with hope, only to have it cruelly dashed by a large red sign that red, 'A303 CLOSED', frustrated, I continued, and eventually found the M27 to Poole, and from there I could pick up the Dorchester road and straight into Exeter on the A35.

Chris was fast asleep, but my hopes were raised as I saw the blue motorway sign for M27. I had spent an extra hour trying to negotiate my way to getting to the south west. I had only travelled a few minutes when further along the M27 a large notice read 'CLOSED'. I swore out loud which woke up Chris, 'are we there yet?' he asked. I did not bother answering, but was getting worried now.

I had travelled too far down south to return to London and pick up the M4, but it was just as well I did not do that, because I found out later that the M4 was also closed south because of a nasty motor car accident. Affectively all major routes to the south west was shut, and I had been on the road for nearly three hours, the time was nearly two am in the morning. I said to Chris, who was half asleep at this point, that if I could not find an alternative route quickly then I would give up, pull up in a layby and go to sleep.

But, as luck would have it, a large B & Q lorry who had been driving in front of me, indicated, turned off the M27, and I followed him closely, all around a large town, I have no idea of its name. I was taken on a tour around an industrial estate, when I had nearly given up, and just about to pull in to get some sleep, the sign in front of me, read, 'A35 Dorchester'. The B & Q lorry indicated and turned off for the A 35 Dorchester, it was lucky I followed the lorry.

A few minutes later after a huge sigh of relief from both me and Chris, I heard a loud bang at the back of my car, and the steering became difficult, a red warning light came on the dash board of Chris's BMW. 'What is that?' I asked Chris pointing to the warning light that was showing some sort of red semi circle. Chris leaned over, rubbed his eyes, yawned, and said, 'well, I have seen it come on before, but I can't remember what it is for, not much I think,' he said, and returned to sleep.

I continued driving, not thinking of the unthinkable, fed up, tired, and just wanting my bed. When we arrived back in Devon at just gone three am in the morning, Chris and I went straight to our beds, without unpacking, or washing, and left everything where it was.

It was only in the morning when I went to unload the car, that I noticed a flat rear tyre. I called Chris and showed him the tyre, and he said, 'ah I remember, yes that warning light it is for a puncture. That light came on when I had a puncture, I thought I had seen it somewhere before.'

Later that morning, after only a few hours sleep, I got dressed in my bee protective suit and went to inspect my bees that I had neglected for the last couple of weeks.

I have decided from comparing my reading around on the subject of bees, and from watching the bee farmer working on his bees, and that dreadful man from the Bee

Association, that the best way for me to observe my own bees is from the outside of the hive. This would be less stressful to the bees, and would not put them back a couple of days, when hives are smoked, opened, and examined, the bees hate this, and the beekeeper can only do so much to the bees when he has looked inside. It is like digging up a plant, shaking its roots free of dirt, looking at it, and then placing it back in the ground, a similar principle can be applied when sticking your hands inside the colony and pulling up frames of bees on them, and shaking the bees roughly off the frames, not good as far as I am concerned and you should only go into the hive when absolutely necessary.

I stand to the right of the bee hives, close up and without smoking the bees and without my bee protective suit on, and from there I watch the bees working. I am learning to assess whether or not all is well with the colony, what is going on as they fly in and out of their hives.

However, my purpose later that morning, and dressed in the gear, which seemed to impress my son, whose comment were 'all dressed in the gear, with no idea,' as I walked into the house wearing my suit. He was closer to the truth then he realized, and I of course did not let on, that I had only a small idea of what I was observing.

But, my purpose was to take a peak inside the hive and find out whether or not my bees had made any extra honey in the supers, I had put on the hives just before I left for

Aldershot. But, to my disappointment and also to my son's who loves honey, and was hoping to take some back with him to Dubai, there were no filled in frames of honey.

After my son went off to visit his friends in Crediton that he had not seen for over a year, I drove a sixty mile round trip to Okehampton to buy some Devonshire honey with the label removed from my bee supply shop, to pass off as my own honey to my son. I did not want to admit defeat in the honey production side of my beekeeping, as my son had kindly pointed out to me that I could have bought an awful lot of expensive honey for the price I had paid for all my bees and equipment. But, he does not understand that this is not the point of beekeeping, beekeeping is much more than producing honey. It is learning about the science of honey bees, and how everything is connected to nature, and our environment, and about living and life.

I just love standing and watching my bees, and slowly I am learning from them. I know the queen is inside the colony and laying the eggs for baby bees, and for the colony to grow and expand. I can tell this by the young bees flying from the hive for the first time. The new bees always do an orientation flight before flying off, so then can get their bearing. I can also tell if the queen is in the colony, because the worker bees bring back pollen and nectar in their sacks which I can see, lately it has been white sacks, this is from the blackberry bushes. The pollen and nectar produce honey, so I am happy that the bees are not being starved inside their hives, which can happen in the June gap when food source is not plentiful as the spring months. The pollen also means that the grubs inside the colony are being fed, and that the queen must be inside to have laid the eggs for the grubs to develop.

I can also tell if all is well just from the sound of the hives. When the colony is working as it should, the bees make a soft humming noise, either because they are fanning the honey cells to reduce the humidity, or fanning the queen to keep her cool on hot days. A loud angry buzzing sound is not good, and can mean that the colony is ready to swarm, or there are to many drones, and no queen inside. Either way, there is in my book, nothing much I can do about this anyway, and just hope that the colony can sort themselves out, by either producing a good egg laying queen and get rid of the drones.

I left the two jars of honey that cost me five pounds each in my son's room, all bubble wrapped ready to be packed off to Dubai. I cheated, I know I did, but hey he won't realize that it is not my honey bees that produce those two jars of honey. Not unless he reads this, but he won't, life in Dubai is far more exciting then to read about beekeeping.

Chapter 16
Robbers
16th July

Dear Shelagh,

Keeping bees is really fascinating, especially since lately, I have taken to spending many hours watching the bees working. I have an upturned galvanised bucket which I sit upon, just a few feet away from the hive entrance, and it is from there that I am able to watch the coming and goings of my bee colonies.

After my son returned to Dubai I had more time to spend watching my bees. I expect my neighbours have concerns that I have totally lost the plot, when I sit perfectly still on an upturned bucket at the end of my garden, holding a blue fishing net in my right hand, and every so often I lean over the front of the hive scoop something off and then proceed to violently stamp on the ground.

There is an explanation for my odd behaviour, which I shall explain, and it is all to do with robbers. My reading around has paid off for my beekeeping practices, because I quickly realized that something was radically wrong with the right hand hive, the one that swarmed earlier in the year and leaving behind a smaller colony of bees.

The entrance to the hive was still wide open, I had been advised to open up the entrance so the bees can fly in and out quickly, and therefore, produce more honey. But, to my horror there were quite a few dead bees lying around the entrance to the hive. I stood around for a few minutes watching, and then the robbers came, four of them, the yellow jacket robbers, who buzzed loudly around me, then zig zagged towards the entrance and entered, a few seconds later, a couple of honey bees flew out fighting with the wasps. The both fell to the ground, and both wasp and bees were dead.

The guards at the entrance of the colony fight to the death to protect their colony, and I had just witness such behaviour. It was heartbreaking watching this little colony of bees dwindle in front of my eyes as they fought so ferociously to protect their queen, and their very existence. I ran back up the garden, and googled frantically to find a solution to this problem. Some of my books mentioned a problem of wasps robbing, but none had a solution. But, alarmingly according to my books, the problem of wasps attacking a hive is dangerous to the bees, who can become seriously depleted and left to die from either fighting to the death, or staved because their honey has gone.

My research on the internet suggested a wet bed sheet hung over the hive, apparently the honey bees could find the entrance underneath the sheet, but the wasps could not. I rang my bee suppliers, and a wasps catcher was recommended as a good and efficient way to catch the wasps.

Later that morning, I drove over to Okehampton to collect my wasp catcher, which was quite disappointing to say the least. It was nothing more than a yellow plastic container with a hole in the middle. I was told to put beer in the container, because wasps love beer but my honeybees do not. I left the bee suppliers fifteen pound and ten pence lighter in my purse, after I purchased the wasps catcher at ten pounds, and a further jar of honey for myself at five pounds and ten pence.

I sent Colin off to the local pub for some left over beer, he walked slowly back carrying the wasp catcher full of beer. I hung the plastic container full of sweet smelling beer over the fence near the hive and went off in search of a much needed cup of tea. I did not want to stay around long enough to witness the death of wasps by drowning. I felt really bad about hanging the contraption up on the fence.

It was a few hours later when I inspected the plastic wasp catcher, to find inside not a wasp but one of my bees, dead. I felt dreadful killing the bee. I had to think of an alternative plan, and removed the offending much expensive wasp catcher (not), away and back into the house.

I vaguely remembered reading somewhere that protect a small vulnerable colony it was advised to make the entrance hole smaller to the front of the hive using grass. I walked back down the garden, gathered handfuls of grass and stuffed it into the entrance, leaving just enough space for one bee to come in and out. I placed Colin on guard, where he sat on the bucket and watched the bee situation for me. 'A nice easy job San,' Colin said smiling, and 'the bees leave me alone.'

But, sadly this did not work, the wasps were finding small gaps between the grass and getting into the hive. I had to think of yet another plan to foil these robbers. Searching in my shed, I found some foam, and cut this into thin strips, and without any smoke, or my bee protection suit, I knelt in front of the hive and gingerly placed the strips into the opening. Two bees came out to inspect my work, and walked along my ungloved fingers. I froze, this was not in my plan. I was unprotected and waiting patiently to be stung.

I was lucky, the bees bored with my fingers went back inside their hive, followed by a wasp. I swore.

I left Colin still at the entrance of the hive, just a few feet away, enough so he can view the hive, but not disturb the bees. The bees seem to know what is an acceptable distance away from their hive, they are extremely clever. Only this time Colin was armed with a rolled up newspaper, the Sun, I think, some old paper I found in the shed after the tenant had rented the property from my son.

I went upstairs to check on Tweety my little bird, and where I have a grandstand view of the garden, the hives and Colin, who was waving the newspaper in the air. It must have been a strange sight to my neighbours, an upturned bucket, a yellow plastic container dangling from a fence, and a Colin swinging wildly in the air with a newspaper all down the bottom of my garden.

Tweety my little rescued Greenfinch is looking her twelve years now. I am surprised that she is able to still keep going, especially with her bad leg, her left eye went last year. It cost me a small fortune at the vets to try and save it, but with no luck. Only now her right eye is also going, she can hardly see. She no longer flies, no longer has her bird bath, and just recently I have to lift her up and place her near her water bottle so she can drink. She does find her food ok, and enjoys her organic piece of apple, and from time to time, I hear her singing, so for now, I am letting nature takes its course with Tweety, but I realize each day I have with her is a huge bonus now. I am not sure she will survive her next moult, when this takes so much out of a healthy young fit bird, not sure how an old bird will cope with it.

After giving Tweety a drink of water, and a bath, whereby I have to physically lift her up and place her in her yellow bath, and position her on her perch to drink. She use to take ages in her bird bath splashing around, these days just a few seconds is all she can manage on her one leg. I went downstairs and rescued Colin. 'Its working,' Colin said, 'but we need a net to catch the wasps in.' Colin rushed off to purchase a blue fishing come butterfly net, it took several hours to locate one, something that I remember having as a child to catch butterflies. But, these days it was not easy to find one.

The blue butterfly net bought, Colin at the ready, which was leaning over the hive, I left him to it. But, from the leaps of shouting, and yelling, he was getting his catch. But, I have a problem with this. I have never killed any creature in my life. I am a vegetarian, and even pick up snails on wet days when they are in the middle of the road, and place them in the hedge so they do not get squashed. I never kill flies, instead I use a glass and paper to remove them safely and let them free outside. So, to hear Colin swooping in joy as he caught the robbers, and stamp on them in the net, was mixed feelings for me.

I knew that each wasp he caught, was one of my bees saved, and their honey stores saved, but it was a death for the wasp. If I did not kill the wasps, then a bee will die fighting it, and if the bees die and the robbers get in then the whole colony would die. It seemed justifiable on the grounds that one wasp killed was saving a lot of bees, and killing them outright with Colin's boots, was also more humane, at least the wasp was not drowning, and therefore taking longer to die in the yellow plastic wasp catcher.

So far the total wasp death count has run into the thirties, a lot of wasps. Colin counts each one he has killed, and stacks them piled up for me to see when I go down to the hive. It is not a pleasant sight, but at least it work. However, there are days, many of them in fact, when Colin or myself cannot be stationed outside the hive, and then the bees have to defend their colony themselves. I hope that we have helped them a little bit to survive. I do wonder how bee farmers manage with wasps, when they have at least forty two hives and more. Do they advertise for jobs vacant in the local newspaper, with the description, 'must stand next to hive, do not move, and swipe any wasps going into hive with net, then stamp on the buggers with a large boot, preferably size nine. Wages are based on the body count.'

Chapter 17

The dilemma of Killing Wasps

18th July

Dear Shelagh,

These last few days Colin and I have taken it in turns to stand guard and swipe any wasps we see with the blue butterfly net and kill them. It is a strange hobby to say the least, and since my beekeeping, I have manage to kill a lot of creatures, my own bees, wasps, and many flies that got trapped in the wasp catcher, not to mention the months in the bee hives.

I am a vegetarian with strict ethical views on not eating or killing anything that has a life, so far my killing spree has gone into overdrive where the wasps are concerned. Colin mistook one of my bees for a wasp as I was approaching him, and before I could scream out not to kill it, too late a size nine boot squashed it.

I had another go at reading one of my many books on beekeeping, looking for anything on robbing in bee hives. I found a small section just past the honey harvesting, which I had missed, because I have not got that far in harvesting my own honey in my beekeeping, instead I am leaving the honey for my own bees, I had missed that bit on wasps further on in the book. I found the section after returning to the back page and looking up the glossary on words.

There it was 'wasps page 143', I hurriedly flicked through the pages of my book, until I reached page 143, and with hope and with my breath held, I eagerly read through the pages hoping that now at long last there was a solution to the wasp robbing problem, and my days of sitting on an upturned bucket at the end of the garden brandishing a blue butterfly net were over, and I could get on with the rest of my life.

There it was, 'wasps', I read the section, 'robbing can be a major problem for bee colonies, it can cause a hive to be depleted and die out, unfortunately there is nothing we can do about it, but hope the bees can defend their colony,' and if that wasn't enough, I read on further, 'there is also the problem of woodpeckers, the green variety who will peck a hole on the side of a bee hive and suck out the honey, and the bees as well, this can also deplete the bee colony.' I swore under my breath, this beekeeping malarkey was not at all how I envisage. I had hope that leaving bee hives at the bottom of the garden with a causal glance now and again would be all it takes. But, after reading the section on wasps, I realized that bees have a huge army of foes, wanting to destroy them, and if that was not all, when I turned over the page, it went on about mice becoming a problem, and badgers, not to mention the foreign hornets.

Bears are a huge problem when it comes to bee hives, who will kick them over to get at the honey. The book advised to erect an electric fence, but this does not always work, depending on how desperate the bears are. So thankfully, we do not have bears in this country to worry about, just wasps, mice, woodpeckers, (green sort), and badgers, so that at least was a plus point.

I was beginning to wonder just how did the honey bees manage to survive all those years with so many robbers after their honey, and now man has added to their pressure to survive. After the passage on wasps in my book, I wandered back down the garden armed with my blue butterfly net to stamp out the wasps, thankfully I only have two hives, any more, and it could be a full time job protecting the bees from their enemies.

A storm is brewing just off the coast, the hot, humid air, is turning thick, and the wind has got up, not a cool breeze but something similar to that in Dubai, a hot air sort of breeze. The bees hate thunderstorms, they become frantic in their foraging. They are not able to hear the weather forecast so stock pile on the honey just in case the storm is here to last. The honeybees are an amazing creature, they are able to predicate the weather and make plans, just like they do for the seasons.

Chapter 18
Tweety's Passing
19th June

Dear Shelagh,

    I was dreading the day when I would lose little Tweety, my rescue Greenfinch, but sadly the day came and no matter how much I had prepared myself to cope with her death, it was such a difficult time. I only noticed last month, how Tweety did not fly to her top perch in her cage, where her water bottle is situated. Instead she would spend much of her time on the floor of her cage.

    When I gently lifted Tweety up to examine her, I noticed with horror her right eye was a deep red and she constantly rubbed her head on her perch. When I spoke to her she would lift her head, and flap her wings, in her usual greeting to me, but then her head would slowly droop as though she had no strength in her neck to support her head.

    She would still eat her slice of organic apple at the bottom of her cage and flick her seeds out of her bowl until she came to her favourites sun flower seeds, and hemp seeds.

And, she still made a slight noise not a whistling sound like she use to, or a twittering sound, but a slight noise, as though calling me back into her room, something she had always done, and I would return, and sit by her cage and talk to her once again, and make my clucking noise with my tongue. It is the sound she is use to since a fledgling all those years ago, when I found her after that stormy August morning, with no feathers. Hard to believe that was thirteen years ago, and thirteen years of closely sharing my bedroom and my life.

I never thought she would live, and I remember the hard work handing feed her on my lap, holding her gently between my fingers using a pair of tweezers dropping wet kitten food into her gapping mouth every two hours, ten hours a day, until she could peck the seeds herself.

She made her slight funny noise this morning after I left her room, and after placing a fresh piece of apple in her cage, she had not done this for sometime. Something inside of me told me to go back to her, and I spent longer than usual sitting beside her. I just knew in my heart that my time was short, precious, and limited. I had feeling she was not in good health. Only last year I had tried to save her left eye by taking her to the vets twice.

It was not easy administering eye drops to such a small eye, and the sad thing was she still lost the sight in her eye, and that was when she stopped flying around my bedroom, or stopped flying towards me to perch on my head and give me bird therapy. She did this by gently grooming me, making feel so relaxed and happy to be in her company. She often dived bomb me, and flew and perched on the door handle not allowing me to leave my bedroom, she had her funny little ways.

She filled an enormous hole in my life. Such a tiny bird, but gave so much too me, and when I looked at her in the cage this morning, I did something I had not done for a long time. I picked her up gently and sat her on my lap, she flapped her wings at me, gapped at me, and then settled down on my lap. But, her head hung low, and I looked down at her and felt such a wrench in my stomach, she would be leaving me soon.

I placed her in back in the cage, her red eye looked so painful. 'What shall I do?' I asked more to myself than to Tweety, 'please let me know. Someone give me a sign.' I did not think I had the right to take her to the vets, because I knew what the outcome would be, and who was I to take her life, surely nature would let her go when her time was up. That was what I had always wished for, just to let nature take its course, not me. Please don't let me make that decision to end her life.

But, I could not let her suffer, I had no right to do that. To let her live in pain, was keeping her for myself, and not to make me suffer the hurt I knew dam well I would feel when she left me, because she was my life too, she had shared so much with me. Tweety had shared my heartache and pain through life's traumas and she was with me, comforting me, giving me bird therapy. She would be gone, and 'what then?' I asked myself. Would I have the strength to cope when she was the one giving me the strength to carry on with life, and the shit it often brings with it. I placed Tweety in her cage, and looked to the sky outside, a grey evening, with the threat of heavy rain, and I asked for a sign, any sign for me to do the right thing, because I was not sure what the right decision was.

I rang the vet, and was told to bring her straight up, and the vet would wait for me, it would have to be emergency after hours service, because the veterinary surgery was closing soon. I knew that it would be expensive, but I also knew that the cost did not matter to me, all the mattered was Tweety's well-being.

I grabbed a box and gently placed Tweety inside it, and she sat next to me on my twenty minute drive to Crediton and to the vets. All the time, my heart sank, and I felt such pain, knowing in my heart Tweety's fate.

The vet was waiting at the door for me, and I went straight into the room, and within minutes of the vet examining Tweety, he confirmed my fears. She was suffering, and given her age, thirteen in August, she would be blind in both eyes soon, and she was weak, very weak, she was slowly losing her life, but painfully.

I signed my name on the piece of paper giving permission for Tweety to be put to sleep. I spent a few minutes holding her warm, small, body, her smell, that bird seed fresh hay sort of smell, she was quiet. She would soon be at peace and free from pain. But, her lost was a devastating lost for me, I wanted to die too, the pain inside was too great for me to cope with. The receptionist was pleasant, and asked if I wanted a drink of water, but they did not understand just how much this little bird meant to me. I gave her, her life, I cared for her, she gave me the will to live. She was not like any other pet I had, she was much more than that.

I sat in the car, only for a few minutes, until the vet came out and handed me the small box, he said she went quickly, and he had wrapped her up. I put the box on the front seat, and drove home through a cloud of tears, that ran freely ran down my face, and I wanted to scream out, 'why, why.' Who creates and then takes away life, and what reason had I to live now, I felt like finishing it as well, wishing the vet had taken me too. So my pain would end. I knew I was a mess. Messed up inside, and hurting like hell.

I left Tweety in the car when I got home, I could not bring myself to take her out, and like a robot I moved through the house taking her cage outside and placed it in the front garden next to the gate, the rain was pouring, and I was soaked. Her blankets over cage that she had on at night, I opened the bedroom window and threw them outside. I could not bare the reminder of her not being there any more. I did take her branch out of her cage, the one I found for her thirteen years ago. I took the branch and place it inside my wardrobe.

As I removed bags and packets from my cupboard, it struck me just how much stuff I had for such a tiny bird. There was sandpaper, grit, bath, drinking bottle, and her seed bowl, not to mention all the different types of seeds around the house. There was also her fresh sprigs of millet that I recently bought for her, which I threw over the fence for the chickens, who also had her bowl of seeds.

I did all this, removing Tweety's stuff with a broken heart, and with tears running down my face. I felt a massive hole had ripped through me, my grief, my pain, it was and still is so raw. The worst part, is not hearing her gently shuffling around in her cage at night, that comforting sound of another living creature sharing my bedroom with me. Her small presence was such a source of comfort, it stopped my loneliness.

After the removal of all Tweety's things my room felt hollow and empty, it was stark. There was no cage at the bottom of my bed, no red blanket to cover her at night, and no small table for her cage to sit on. I had removed it all, apart from her white plastic bath, that I left in my own bath. I found sleep difficult, and kept thinking of Tweety outside in my car. She was gone.

Chapter 19

When my Granddaughter made a Coffin

20th June

Dear Shelagh,

    For the first time in thirteen years my little radio was not switch on, normally I switch it on for Tweety, she enjoyed listening to radio two, she would whistle along to the music. Switching the radio on was the first thing I did every morning. It was part of my routine, and for the first time in thirteen years, I did not have to cut up a piece of organic apple for her, or fill her water bottle, or replace the seeds in her bowl. For the first time in thirteen years, my routine was different. Normally Tweety gets cleaned first thing in the morning, she is fed, and radio two put on, but not this morning, instead where her cage normally sits, there was nothing. There was no apple to cut. I sat at the end of my bed and stared hard at the empty space where once a cage sat, now only a handful of small feathers lay on the carpet, there would be no small, warm, sweet, smelling body to snuggle up to my ear, and pull gently on my hair.

For the first time in thirteen years something was missing, and I would not be walking into my bedroom, and sit with her like I use to. I would often during the day or evening pop into see Tweety, where we would sit together, her presence a great source of comfort to me, now I had no reason to keep opening my bedroom door, and slide around the side of her cage. Once or twice today I thought I heard her tweeting to me, and once or twice I forgot, and expected to still see her sitting on the window sill whistling to me.

For the first time in thirteen years I could wear my pyjamas. I could not wear them when Tweety shared my bedroom, she hated any bright colours, and patterns, she would fly from perch to perch tweeting intensely, telling me off, showing her displeasure. I would then remove any item of clothing that offended her and rush to reassure her.

I never use to believe in fate, until this morning. I was on my way over to my friend Colin's flat, and the first thing I heard on the radio this morning was Sting on Radio Two, with 'If you Love somebody set them free.' That was it, that was my sign. I had set my bird free from pain and suffering because I love her.

The rest of the day was a strange day, a day so wrecked in pain, even though I had my little granddaughter Phoebe over for the day, it was still hard to cope with the loss of my bird. Colin my friend had brought Tweety out of my car, and placed her in the cat basket at the back of the shed, ready for her burial, something we both wanted to do.

The pieces of wood were hammered together by Phoebe, she found the right nails, and when asked handed the nails to Colin, and then both of them would hammer the nails into the wood, until a small box had taken shape. I then dug a hole in the new wild flower section in the garden, just by the fence, and close to where I found her all those years ago. There the little box with Tweety inside resting on hay, and wrapped in tissue was laid to rest.

Phoebe had no idea, and I could not tell her, besides she is only two years old. She just had fun hammering the nails into the wood, and watching a box taking shape. And, later that evening when I took her back home, her father asked if she had fun. I replied she had great fun, and that Phoebe had enjoyed making a coffin. I knew her father wasn't listening to me, when he said, 'oh good,' and went back to the business of cooking tea over the noise of the television, and the children's programme drowning out any other conversation that could have taken place, but didn't. Instead, I chose to leave, my child care duties at an end, and I returned home and to my empty bedroom, and empty life, and wondered if I could carry on.

As I drew the curtains over the window later that evening, the rain clouds had disapeared, hurrying over Dartmoor, and the light from the moon fell across the small square patch in the wild flower garden, and over the plaque I bought, that read, 'in memory of a friend'. The words on the plaque were not quite what I had wanted, but it was the nearest I could find in the local garden centre. It should have read, 'in memory of someone special in my life never forgotten.'

My dear friend David, suggested over coffee that I should buy another bird. But, that will never happen, Tweety was a one off, a bird that literally fell into my life. I do not believe in having a cage bird as a pet, and Tweety was special, she did not know of any other way of life, and had been raised by hand by me, and had imprinted on me. There will be no other bird in my life.

I did something else that evening, that I could not normally do, and that was being able to read in bed, something that I could not have done with Tweety in my room. I would try switching the bedside table light on, only to hear a cross shuffling and moaning from the cage, and if I was not quick enough to switch the light out, she would fly angry from perch to perch, and afraid that she would hurt herself, I would hurriedly switch the light off and try and sleep, or at least wait until the shuffling stopped and Tweety was once again settled in her cage.

So for the first time in thirteen years, I picked up a book, and read on observing the entrance to the hive. My bees for now would take some of my time, where Tweety had previously filled.

Since observing from the entrance of the bee hive, my bees have stayed friendly, no nasty buzzing or following down the garden. They are happy enough for me to stand close to their hives and watch them. They often buzz my head, or fly into my neck, as I do have to stand directly in their flight path to observe them, but they must shake themselves free from my hair, shake their wings, and fly off. There is no painful stings to follow from the temporary landing in my hair, or neck. I am pleasantly surprise, and so too is my friend Colin. It is such a privilege to be watching my bees so closely, without either of us wearing a protective suit.

I feel they have got to know me, and trust me, and realize that I pose no threat to their colony, and have no intentions of prising open their home, and digging around inside. I can see all I need to see just by watching them.

I did open up the top super the other morning to take peak inside, and only gently smoked it, just a few puffs, and the girls came to the top to greet me, took a walk around the outside of the super, and allowed me to peer inside. I then gently brushed the top few bees off, and closed up their home. They were happy, I was happy, and I let the bees do what bees do best, take care of themselves.

Chapter 20

I lost my best friend and my companion today.

2nd August

Dear Shelagh,

    I was never expecting this. It really came out of the blue, a total shock. I just thought my Standard Poodle would go on for ever, always by my side, always with me on my travels and walks, so it came as such a horrible shock when she suddenly left me. My sister had just arrived from Louth in Lincolnshire to help me with my decorating. We were both going to get stuck into my bedroom, rip the old wallpaper off the walls, and give my room a lick of paint to liven it up, instead of the dull brown wallpaper that had been on the walls since moving into the house thirteen years ago, and in its place a beautiful sea lavender was going to be painted. I wanted to create something special in my bedroom, like a mellow calmness it deserved. So that I may sit and enjoy the spectacular views over the valley.

Somehow things have a habit of not quite going to plan, all the bedroom painting went out of the window, the following day. The previous evening it had turned out to be a beautiful summers evening, after my sister turned up, and wishing to recover from her horrendous journey down the M5, she suggested a walk up over Randon top, where the views span out across to both Dartmoor and Exmoor. Its really like walking on top of the world.

It was still early when we left for our walk with the dogs, but first we had to drive up the long hill, and park close to the top of the hill, along a small lane. This was because my old Poodle struggled to walk, her legs were arthritic, but Teigan my thirteen year old Standard Poodle always enjoyed this walk, so many sniffs and best of all she could run free, doing her own thing.

The views from Randon are outstanding that even my son who is constantly plugged into his phone, manage for a few minutes to stand in awe at the scenery that panned out in front of him, a panoramic view that catches the breath, and makes one feel on top of the world and alive.

My sister and I helped Teigan out of the car, she found getting in and out difficult, but once out she appeared a lot easier in her moments. Little Erik dog ran ahead sniffing out rabbits, followed closely by Teigan who seemed to have a new lease of life, in fact my sister commented on how good Teigan looked for her age. A sprightly poodle, greying around the mouth, deaf, and losing her sight, but still gave a small half hearted chase after Erik, who both lingered around the tempting rabbit holes, with no bunnies in sight, but plenty to sniff about. We only walked about fifteen minutes, mostly we stood and stared to the distance Exmoor, which was definitely having a torrential downpour, the sky was thundery black over in that direction, and even as we stood watching the storm developing, we could feel a sudden drop in temperature, and the wind began to pick up. The storm was moving towards us across the hill tops, and would not be long before we were under it.

We made a fairly hasty retreat to the car, and the dogs settled down in the back, not entirely bothered, nor out of breath from running. Teigan held her head up high and gazed out through the back seat window, she always did this. We always joked that this was her reflected moment, she had many of these in her life, a wise old dog she was.

The following morning occurred in a haze of pain and tears, when I quickly realised that during the night Teigan had a massive stroke and was paralysed. Her body was limp, her breathing shallow, and her eyes were dull, nothing behind them. She was laid out across the sofa, not moving, not even lifting her head. Her eyes held a plea within them, to let her go.

Both my sister and I cried as we carried her limp body between us, this large heavy poodle to the car, and gently laid her on the back seat, wrapped up in a blanket. The drive to the vets was painful, the windscreen wipers desperate to catch the lashing rain, was the only sound in the car. Neither my sister or I spoke during the twenty minute journey to the vets. We knew this was Teigan's last car journey.

The vet came out to the car and examined Teigan, and a few minutes later she shook her head. It was the kindest thing to let her go, this beautiful dog was no longer able to move.

I hugged Teigan rubbing my face in her woolly coat, as the vet held her in her arms and carried her into the surgery, my sister went with her. I stayed by the car, the rain was lashing down, it mixed with my tears, my heart was breaking, the pain so deep, that I had to restrain myself from running after them, rushing into the room and snatching my dog back. A few minutes later my sister came out holding Teigan's collar, a brown thin leather collar, she handed it to me. I realized my companion, and loyal friend had gone.

The pain was pure, and raw, still is, and an overwhelming sense of emptiness entered my life, because my life had been full up to that point, full of my dog, a big dog, that I would trip over in the kitchen, the living room, and my bedroom, big brown eyes that would follow me around, and in times of upsets in my life, I would lie with her, my face crushed into her black curly fur and cry, and she would lay perfectly still allowing me the moment to weep.

This would never happen again, she was gone, she had left me, and left a hole in my life, unfulfillable, a massive void, no walks with my big dog, who made me felt safe, no drives with her big eyes staring at me in the mirror, no big ear washes with her lizard like tongue, or licks, no greetings to meet me, no big welcome home, nothing can give you a welcome home like a dog, even family members cannot display that pure delight at your return home, when you have left them behind. Whether it is for a few minutes apart, hours or days, that welcome home is always the same, bouncing in pure delight that the head of the pack has returned.

The decorating was put on hold, instead, cups of coffee and weeping became the norm, until my sister returned home quickly, mainly because she too found it too much, when Teigan returned home the following day from the vets, in the back of the car, covered in a blanket and then carried through to the garden and placed in a large hole in the wild flower section of the garden. My friend Colin had built a wall around her grave. 'I hugged her to the end,' my sister said, 'and she slipped peacefully away.'

My bees have been left to their own devices, first Tweety left me, followed within a fortnight by Teigan my dog. My life has been shattered, and nothing has any meaning any more, my heart is not in beekeeping. I wander around in a daze, thinking about ending my life, slipping peacefully away to join my companions. Colin did say that the robbing wasps were back and asked me, if he should use his blue butterfly net to catch and kill them. I replied, 'no. There have been to many deaths,' I said, 'leave the bees alone, let them sort it out.'

Printed in Great Britain
by Amazon